The Beatles Lyrics.

ISBN 0-7935-1537-8

HAL•LEONARD®
CORPORATION
7777 W. BLUEMOUND RD. P.O. BOX 13819 MILWAUKEE, WI 53213

Visit Hal Leonard Online at
www.halleonard.com

Book design by Pearce Marchbank.

Photographs Front cover: Norman Parkinson/Hamiltons Photographers.
Text photos: Tom Blau/Camera Press;197:Camera Press;77,127:Robert
Freeman/Camera Press; 45,107:Frank Hermann/Camera Press;145,156:
Howard/Camera Press;63:J.Lannois /Camera Press;52:Bruce McBroom/Camera
Press;213:Terry O'Neill/Camera Press;163:Thomas Picton/Camera Press;114: Rex
Features;66,71,131,166:Terence Spencer/ Camera Press;31,37.

Printed and bound in Great Britain by Bath Press Colourbooks, Glasgow.

Discography

*This discography is of all British Beatles recordings in the order of their release.
All CDs released up to publication of this book are also indicated.
The singer of each song is shown in brackets. Album and EP titles, and A-sides are shown in bold.
Titles not written by the Beatles are, of course, not included in the lyric section of this book. For
copyright reasons, the lyrics of the reconstructed songs 'Free As A Bird' and 'Real Love'
are not featured in this book.*

1962.

Love Me Do (Paul)/
P.S. I Love You (Paul)
PARLOPHONE R 4949. PRODUCED: GEORGE MARTIN
RELEASED: OCTOBER 5 1962
RE-RELEASED AS PARLOPHONE CD3R 4949, NOVEMBER 1988

1963.

Please Please Me (John)/
Ask Me Why (John)
PARLOPHONE R 4983. PRODUCED: GEORGE MARTIN
RELEASED JANUARY 12, 1963
RE-RELEASED AS PARLOPHONE CD3R 4983, NOVEMBER 1988

From Me To You (John and Paul)/
Thank You Girl (John and Paul)
PARLOPHONE R 5015. PRODUCED: GEORGE MARTIN
RELEASED: APRIL 11, 1963
RE-RELEASED AS PARLOPHONE CD3R 5015, NOVEMBER 1988

'Please Please Me'
PARLOPHONE PCS 3042. PRODUCED: GEORGE MARTIN
RELEASED: APRIL 1963
RE-RELEASED PARLOPHONE CDP7 464352, FEBRUARY 1987
I Saw Her Standing There (Paul)/
Misery (John and Paul)/Anna (John)
Chains (George)/Boys (Ringo)/
Ask Me Why (John)/
Please Please Me (John)/
Love Me Do (Paul)/
P.S. I Love You (Paul)/Baby It's You (John)/
Do You Want To Know A Secret? (George)/
A Taste Of Honey (Paul)/
There's A Place (John and Paul)/
Twist And Shout (John)

She Loves You (John and Paul)/
I'll Get You (John and Paul)

PARLOPHONE R 5055. PRODUCED: GEORGE MARTIN
RELEASED: AUGUST 23, 1963
RE-RELEASED AS PARLOPHONE CD3R 5055, NOVEMBER 1988

'The Beatles' Hits'

PARLOPHONE GEP 8880. PRODUCED GEORGE MARTIN
RELEASED: SEPTEMBER 1963

From Me to You/Thank You Girl/
Please Please Me/Love Me Do

'Twist And Shout'

PARLOPHONE GEP 8882. PRODUCED: GEORGE MARTIN
RELEASED: SEPTEMBER 1963

Twist And Shout/A Taste Of Honey/
Do You Want To Know A Secret?/
There's A Place

I Want To Hold Your Hand (John and Paul)/
This Boy (John and Paul)

PARLOPHONE R 5084. PRODUCED: GEORGE MARTIN
RELEASED: NOVEMBER 29, 1963
RE-RELEASED AS PARLOPHONE CD3R 5084, JANUARY 1989

'The Beatles No. 1'

PARLOPHONE GEP 8883. PRODUCED: GEORGE MARTIN
RELEASED: NOVEMBER 1963

I Saw Her Standing There/Misery/
Anna/Chains

'With The Beatles'

PARLOPHONE PCS 3045. PRODUCED: GEORGE MARTIN
RELEASED: NOVEMBER 22, 1963
RE-RELEASED AS PARLOPHONE CDP7 46436 2, FEBRUARY 1987

It Won't Be Long (John)/
All I've Got To Do (John)
All My Loving (Paul)/
Don't Bother Me (George)/
Little Child (John)/
Till There Was You (Paul)/
Please Mr Postman (John)/
Roll Over Beethoven (George)/
Hold Me Tight (Paul)/
You Really Got A Hold On Me (John)/
I Wanna Be Your Man (Ringo)/
Devil In Her Heart (George)/
Not A Second Time (John)/Money (John)

1964.

'All My Loving'
PARLOPHONE GEP 8891. PRODUCED: GEORGE MARTIN
RELEASED: FEBRUARY 7, 1964

All My Loving/Ask Me Why/Money/P.S. I Love You

Can't Buy Me Love (Paul)/You Can't Do That (John)
PARLOPHONE R 5114. PRODUCED: GEORGE MARTIN
RELEASED: MARCH 20, 1964
RE-RELEASED AS PARLOPHONE CD3R 5114, JANUARY 1989.

'Long Tall Sally'
PARLOPHONE GEP 8913. PRODUCED: GEORGE MARTIN
RELEASED: JUNE 19, 1964

I Call Your Name (John)/
Slow Down (John and Paul)/
Long Tall Sally (Paul)/
Matchbox (Ringo)

A Hard Day's Night (John plus Paul)/
Things We Said Today (Paul)
PARLOPHONE R 5160. PRODUCED: GEORGE MARTIN
RELEASED: JULY 10, 1964
RE-RELEASED AS PARLOPHONE CD3R 5160, FEBRUARY 1989

'A Hard Day's Night'
PARLOPHONE PCS 3058. PRODUCED: GEORGE MARTIN
RELEASED: JULY 10, 1964
RE-RELEASED AS PARLOPHONE CDP7 46437 2, FEBRUARY 1987

A Hard Day's Night (John plus Paul)/
I Should Have Known Better (John)/
If I Fell (John and Paul)/
I'm Happy Just To Dance With You (George)/
And I Love Her (Paul)/
Tell Me Why (John, Paul and George)/
Can't Buy Me Love (Paul)/
Any Time At All (John)/
I'll Cry Instead (John)/
Things We Said Today ()Paul)/
When I Get Home (John)/
You Can't Do That (John)/
I'll Be Back (John and Paul)

I Feel Fine (John)/
She's A Woman (Paul)
PARLOPHONE R 5200. PRODUCED: GEORGE MARTIN
RELEASED: NOVEMBER 27, 1964
RE-RELEASED AS PARLOPHONE CD3R 5200, FEBRUARY 1989

'A Hard Day's Night No. 1'

PARLOPHONE GEP 8920. PRODUCED: GEORGE MARTIN
RELEASED: NOVEMBER 4, 1964

I Should Have Know Better/If I Fell/
Tell Me Why/And I Love Her

'A Hard Day's Night No. 2'

PARLOPHONE GEP 8924. PRODUCED: GEORGE MARTIN
RELEASED: NOVEMBER 6, 1964

Any Time At All/I'll Cry Instead/
Things We Said Today/When I Get Home

'Beatles For Sale'

PARLOPHONE PCS 3062. PRODUCED: GEORGE MARTIN
RELEASED: NOVEMBER 27, 1964
RE-RELEASED AS PARLOPHONE CDP7 464382, 1988

No Reply (John)/I'm A Loser (John)/
Baby's In Black (John plus Paul)/
Rock And Roll Music (John)/
I'll Follow The Sun (Paul)/
Mr Moonlight (John)/Kansas City (Paul)/
Eight Days A Week (John and Paul)/
Words Of Love (John and Paul)/
Honey Don't (Ringo)/
Every Little Thing (John plus Paul)/
I Don't Want To Spoil The Party (John)/
What You're Doing (Paul)/
Everybody's Trying To Be My Baby (George)

1965.

Ticket To Ride (John)/
Yes It Is (John plus Paul)

PARLOPHONE R 5265. PRODUCED: GEORGE MARTIN
RELEASED: APRIL 9, 1965
RE-RELEASED AS PARLOPHONE CD3R 5265, MARCH 1989

'Beatles For Sale No. 1'

PARLOPHONE GEP 8931. PRODUCED: GEORGE MARTIN
RELEASED: APRIL 6, 1965

No Reply/I'm A Loser/
Rock And Roll Music/Eight Days A Week

'Beatles For Sale No. 2'

PARLOPHONE GEP 8938. PRODUCED GEORGE MARTIN
RELEASED: JUNE 4, 1965

I'll Follow The Sun/Baby's In Black/
Words Of Love/
I Don't Want To Spoil The Party

Help! (John)/
I'm Down (Paul)

PARLOPHONE R 5305. PRODUCED: GEORGE MARTIN
RELEASED: JULY 23, 1965

'Help!'

PARLOPHONE PCS 3071. PRODUCED: GEORGE MARTIN
RELEASED: AUGUST 1965
RE-RELEASED AS PARLOPHONE CDP7 46439 2, APRIL 1987

Help! (John)/The Night Before (Paul)/
You've Got To Hide Your Love Away (John)/
I Need You (George)/
Another Girl (Paul)/
You're Gonna Lose That Girl (John)/
Ticket To Ride (John)/
Act Naturally (Ringo)/
It's Only Love (John)/
You Like Me Too Much (George)/
Tell Me What You See (John plus Paul)/
I've Just Seen A Face (Paul)/
Yesterday (Paul)/Dizzy Miss Lizzy (John)

'Rubber Soul'

PARLOPHONE PCS 3075. PRODUCED: GEORGE MARTIN
RELEASED: DECEMBER 3, 1965
RE-RELEASED AS PARLOPHONE CDP7 46440 2, APRIL 1987

Drive My Car (Paul)/
Norwegian Wood (John)/
You Won't See Me (Paul)/
Nowhere Man (John)/
Think For Yourself (Paul)/
The Word (John plus Paul)/Michelle (Paul)/
What Goes On (Ringo)/Girl (John)/
I'm Looking Through You (Paul)/
In My Life (John)/Wait (John plus Paul)
If I Needed Someone (George)/
Run For Your Life (John)

Day Tripper (John plus Paul)/
We Can Work It Out (Paul)

PARLOPHONE R 5389. PRODUCED: GEORGE MARTIN
RELEASED: DECEMBER 3, 1965
RE-RELEASED AS PARLOPHONE CD3R 5389, APRIL 1989

'Beatles Million Sellers'

PARLOPHONE GEP 8946. PRODUCED: GEORGE MARTIN
RELEASED: DECEMBER 5, 1965

She Loves You/I Want To Hold Your Hand/
Can't Buy Me Love/I Feel Fine

1966.

'Yesterday'
PARLOPHONE GEP 8948. PRODUCED: GEORGE MARTIN
RELEASED: MARCH 4, 1966

Act Naturally/You Like Me Too Much/
Yesterday/It's Only Love

Paperback Writer (Paul)/Rain (John)
PARLOPHONE R 5452. PRODUCED: GEORGE MARTIN
RELEASED: JUNE 10, 1966
RE-RELEASED AS PARLOPHONE CD3R 5452, APRIL 1989

'Nowhere Man'
PARLOPHONE GEP 8952. PRODUCED: GEORGE MARTIN
RELEASED: JULY 8, 1966

Nowhere Man/Drive My Car/Michelle/
You Won't See Me

'Revolver'
PARLOPHONE PCS 7009. PRODUCED: GEORGE MARTIN
RELEASED: AUGUST 5, 1966
RE-RELEASED AS PARLOPHONE CDP7 46441 2, APRIL 1987

Taxman (George)/Eleanor Rigby (Paul)/
I'm Only Sleeping (John)/
Love You To (George)/
Here, There And Everywhere (Paul)/
Yellow Submarine (Ringo)/
She Said She Said (John)/
Good Day Sunshine (Paul)/
And Your Bird Can Sing (John)/
For No One (Paul)/Doctor Robert (John)/
I Want To Tell You (George)/
Got To Get You Into My Life (Paul)/
Tomorrow Never Knows (John)

Eleanor Rigby (Paul)/
Yellow Submarine (Ringo)
PARLOPHONE R 5493. PRODUCED: GEORGE MARTIN
RELEASED: AUGUST 8, 1966
RE-RELEASED AS PARLOPHONE CD3R 5493, MAY 1989

'A Collection Of Oldies... But Goldies'
PARLOPHONE PCS 7016. PRODUCED: GEORGE MARTIN
RELEASED: NOVEMBER 1966

She Loves You/From Me To You/
We Can Work It Out/Help!/Michelle/
Yesterday/I Feel Fine/Yellow Submarine/
Can't Buy Me Love/Bad Boy(John)/
Day Tripper/A Hard Day's Night/

Ticket To Ride/Paperback Writer/
Eleanor Rigby/
I Want To Hold Your Hand

1967.

Penny Lane (Paul)/
Strawberry Fields Forever (John)
PARLOPHONE R 5570. PRODUCED: GEORGE MARTIN
RELEASED: FEBRUARY 17, 1967
RE-RELEASED AS PARLOPHONE CD3R 5570, MAY 1988

'Sgt. Pepper's Lonely Hearts Club Band'
PARLOPHONE PCS 7027. PRODUCED: GEORGE MARTIN
RELEASED: JUNE 1, 1967
RE-RELEASED AS PARLOPHONE CDP7 46442 2
Sgt. Pepper's Lonely Hearts Club Band (Paul and John)/
With A Little Help From My Friends (Ringo)/
Lucy In The Sky With Diamonds (John)/
Getting Better (Paul)/Fixing A Hole (Paul)/
She's Leaving Home (Paul)/
Being For The Benefit Of Mr Kite! (John)/
Within You, Without You (George)/
When I'm Sixty Four (Paul)/
Lovely Rita (Paul)/
Good Morning, Good Morning (John)/
A Day In The Life (John and Paul)

All You Need Is Love (John)/
Baby You're A Rich Man (John)
PARLOPHONE R 5620. PRODUCED: GEORGE MARTIN
RELEASED: JULY 7, 1967
RE-RELEASED AS PARLOPHONE CD3R 5620, JUNE 1989.

Hello Goodbye (Paul)/
I Am The Walrus (John)
PARLOPHONE R 5655. PRODUCED: GEORGE MARTIN
RELEASED: NOVEMBER 14, 1967
RE-RELEASED AS PARLOPHONE CD3R 5655, JUNE 1989

'Magical Mystery Tour'
PARLOPHONE SMMT 1/2. PRODUCED: GEORGE MARTIN
RELEASED: DECEMBER 1967
Magical Mystery Tour (John and Paul)/
Your Mother Should Know (Paul)/
I Am The Walrus (John)/
Fool On The Hill (Paul)/
Flying (instrumental)/
Blue Jay Way (George)
RELEASED WITH ADDITIONAL TRACKS IN LP FORMAT AS PCTC 255, DECEMBER 4, 1976.
RE-RELEASED AS PARLOPHONE CDP7 48062 2, OCTOBER 1987

1968.

Lady Madonna (Paul)/
The Inner Light (George)

PARLOPHONE R 5675. PRODUCED: GEORGE MARTIN
RELEASED: MARCH 15, 1968
RE-RELEASED AS PARLOPHONE CD3R 5675, JULY 1989

Hey Jude (Paul)/
Revolution (John)

APPLE R5777. PRODUCED: GEORGE MARTIN
RELEASED: AUGUST 1968
RE-RELEASED AS PARLOPHONE CD3R 5722, JULY 1989

'The Beatles'
(The White Album)

APPLE PCS 7067/7068. PRODUCED: GEORGE MARTIN
RELEASED: NOVEMBER 1968
RE-RELEASED AS PARLOPHONE CD57 464439

Back In The U.S.S.R. (Paul)/
Dear Prudence (John)/Glass Onion (John)/
Ob-La-Di, Ob-La-Da (Paul)/
Wild Honey Pie (Paul)/
The Continuing Story of Bungalow Bill (John)/
While My Guitar Gently Weeps (George)/
Happiness Is A Warm Gun (John)/
Martha My Dear (Paul)/
I'm So Tired (John)/Blackbird (Paul)/
Piggies (George)/Rocky Raccoon (Paul)/
Don't Pass Me By (Ringo)/
Why Don't We Do It In The Road (Paul)/
I Will (Paul)/Julia (John)/Birthday (Paul)
Yer Blues (John)/
Mother Nature's Son (Paul)/
Everybody's Got Something To Hide
Except Me And My Monkey (John)/
Sexy Sadie (John)/Helter Skelter (Paul)/
Long Long Long (George)/
Revolution 1 (John)/Honey Pie (Paul)/
Savoy Truffle (George)/
Cry Baby Cry (John)/
Revolution 9 (instrumental)/
Goodnight (Ringo)

'Yellow Submarine'

APPLE PCS 7070. PRODUCED: GEORGE MARTIN
RELEASED: DECEMBER 1968
RE-RELEASED AS PARLOPHONE CDP7 46445 2

Yellow Submarine (Ringo)/
Only A Northern Song (George)/
All Together Now
(John, Paul, George and Ringo)/
Hey, Bulldog (John)
It's All Too Much (George)/
All You Need Is Love (John)
The other side of the album featured film music
by the George Martin Orchestra

1969.

Get Back (Paul)/
Don't Let Me Down (John)
APPLE R 5777. PRODUCED: GEORGE MARTIN
RELEASED: APRIL 15, 1969
RE-RELEASED AS PARLOPHONE CD3R 5777, AUGUST 1989

The Ballad Of John And Yoko (John)/
Old Brown Shoe (George)
APPLE R 5786. PRODUCED: GEORGE MARTIN
RELEASED: MAY 30, 1969
RE-RELEASED AS PARLOPHONE CD3R 5786, AUGUST 1989

'Abbey Road'
APPLE PCS 7088. PRODUCED: GEORGE MARTIN
RELEASED: SEPTEMBER 26, 1969
RE-RELEASED AS PARLOPHONE CDP7 46446 2, OCTOBER 1987
Come Together (John)/
Something (George)/
Maxwell's Silver Hammer (Paul)/
Oh! Darling (Paul)/
Octopus's Garden (Ringo)/
I Want You – She's So Heavy (John)/
Here Comes The Sun (George)/
Because (John, Paul and George)/
You Never Give Me Your Money (Paul)/
Sun King (John, Paul and George)/
Mean Mr Mustard (Paul)/
Polythene Pam (John)/
She Came In Through The Bathroom Window (Paul)/
Golden Slumbers (Paul)/
Carry That Weight (John, Paul, George and Ringo)/
The End (Paul)/
Her Majesty (Paul)

Something (George)/
Come Together (John)
APPLE R 5814. PRODUCED: GEORGE MARTIN
RELEASED: OCTOBER 31, 1969
RE-RELEASED AS PARLOPHONE CD3R 5814, SEPTEMBER 1989

1970.

Let It Be (Paul)/
You Know My Name (Look Up The Number) (John and Paul)
APPLE 5833. PRODUCED: GEORGE MARTIN
RELEASED: MARCH 6, 1970
RE-RELEASED AS PARLOPHONE CD3R 5833, SEPTEMBER 1989

'Let It Be'
APPLE PCS 7096. PRODUCED: GEORGE MARTIN,
GLYN JOHNS AND PHIL SPECTOR
RELEASED: MAY 8, 1970
RE-RELEASED AS PARLOPHONE CDP7 46447 2, OCTOBER 1987

Two Of Us (John and Paul)/
Dig A Pony (John)/
Across The Universe (John)/
I Me Mine (George)/Dig It (John)/
Let It Be (Paul)/Maggie Mae (John)/
I've Got A Feeling (Paul)/
One After 909 (John and Paul)/
The Long And Winding Road (Paul)/
For You Blue (George)/Get Back (Paul)

1973.

'The Beatles/1962-1966'
APPLE PCSP 717. PRODUCED: GEORGE MARTIN
RELEASED: MAY 5, 1973
RE-RELEASED AS PARLOPHONE BEACD 2511, SEPTEMBER 1993

Love Me Do/Please Please Me/
From Me To You/She Loves You/
I Want To Hold Your Hand/All My Loving/
Can't Buy Me Love/A Hard Day's Night/
And I Love Her/Eight Days A Week/
I Feel Fine/Ticket To Ride/Yesterday/
Help!/You've Got To Hide Your Love Away/
We Can Work It Out/Day Tripper/Drive My Car/
Norwegian Wood/Nowhere Man/Michelle/
In My Life/Girl/Paperback Writer/
Eleanor Rigby/Yellow Submarine

'The Beatles/1967/1970'
APPLE PCSP 718. PRODUCED: GEORGE MARTIN
AND PHIL SPECTOR
RELEASED: MAY 5, 1973
RE-RELEASED AS PARLOPHONE BEACD 2512, SEPTEMBER 1993

Strawberry Fields Forever/Penny Lane
Sgt. Pepper's Lonely Hearts Club Band/
With A Little Help From My Friends/
Lucy In The Sky With Diamonds/A Day In The Life/
All You Need Is Love/I Am The Walrus/Hello Goodbye/
The Fool On The Hill/Magical Mystery Tour/Lady Madonna/
Hey Jude/Revolution/Back In The U.S.S.R./
While My Guitar Gently Weeps/Ob-La-Di, Ob-La-Da/
Get Back/Don't Let Me Down/Ballad Of John And Yoko/
Old Brown Shoe/Here Comes The Sun/
Come Together/Something/Octopus's Garden/
Let It Be/Across The Universe/
The Long And Winding Road

1976.

'Rock 'n' Roll Music'
PARLOPHONE PCSP 719. PRODUCED: GEORGE MARTIN
RELEASED: JUNE 14, 1976
(CURRENTLY UNAVAILABLE ON CD.)

Back In The U.S.S.R./Twist And Shout
PARLOPHONE R 6016. PRODUCED: GEORGE MARTIN
RELEASED: JUNE 25, 1976

1977.

'The Beatles Live! At The Star Club
In Hamburg, Germany: 1962'
LINGASONG LNL1
RELEASED: MAY 1, 1977
(CURRENTLY UNAVAILABLE ON CD.)

'The Beatles At The Hollywood Bowl'
PARLOPHONE EMTV 4. PRODUCED: VOYLE GILMORE
AND GEORGE MARTIN
RELEASED: MAY 6, 1977
(CURRENTLY UNAVAILABLE ON CD.)

'Love Songs'
PARLOPHONE PCSP 721. PRODUCED: GEORGE MARTIN
RELEASED: NOVEMBER 28, 1977
(CURRENTLY UNAVAILABLE ON CD.)

1979.

'Hey Jude'

PARLOPHONE PCS 7184. PRODUCED: GEORGE MARTIN
RELEASED: MAY 1979
(CURRENTLY UNAVAILABLE ON CD.)

'Rarities'

PARLOPHONE PCM 1001. PRODUCED: GEORGE MARTIN
RELEASED: SEPTEMBER 1979
(CURRENTLY UNAVAILABLE ON CD.)

'Beatles Ballads'

PARLOPHONE PCS 7214. PRODUCED: GEORGE MARTIN
RELEASED: OCTOBER 1980
(CURRENTLY UNAVAILABLE ON CD.)

'Rock 'n' Roll Music vol. 1'

MFP 50506. PRODUCED: GEORGE MARTIN
RELEASED: NOVEMBER 1980
(CURRENTLY UNAVAILABLE ON CD.)

'Rock 'n' Roll Music vol. 2'

MFP 50507. PRODUCED: GEORGE MARTIN
RELEASED: NOVEMBER 1980
(CURRENTLY UNAVAILABLE ON CD.)

'Reel Music'

PARLOPHONE PCS 7218. PRODUCED: GEORGE MARTIN
RELEASED: MARCH 1982
(CURRENTLY UNAVAILABLE ON CD.)

'20 Greatest Hits'

PARLOPHONE PCTC 260. PRODUCED: GEORGE MARTIN
RELEASED OCTOBER 1982
(CURRENTLY UNAVAILABLE ON CD.)

'Past Masters Vol. 1'

PARLOPHONE CDBPM1. PRODUCED: GEORGE MARTIN
RELEASED: MARCH 1988

Love Me Do/From Me To You/Thank You Girl/
She Loves You/I'll Get You/I Want To Hold Your Hand/
This Boy/Komm, Gib Mir Deine Hand/Sie Liebt Dich/
Long Tall Sally/I Call Your Name/Slow Down/Matchbox/
I Feel Fine/She's A Woman/Bad Boy/Yes It Is/I'm Down

'Past Masters Vol. 2'

PARLOPHONE CDPM2. PRODUCED: GEORGE MARTIN
RELEASED: MARCH 1988

Day Tripper/We Can Work It Out/Paperback Writer/
Rain/Lady Madonna/The Inner Light/Hey Jude/
Revolution;/Get Back/Don't Let Me Down/
The Ballad Of John and Yoko/Old Brown Shoe/
Across The Universe/Let It Be/
You Know My Name (Look Up The Number)

1994.

'The Beatles Live At The BBC'

APPLE 7243 8 31796 2 6
RELEASED: NOVEMBER 1994

Disc One:

Beatle Greetings (Speech)/From Us To You/Riding On A Bus (Speech)/
I Got A Woman (John)/ Too Much Monkey Business (John)/
Keep Your Hands Off My Baby/I'll Be On My Way (Paul)/Young Blood (George)/
A Shot Of Rhythm And Blues/Sure To Fall (In Love With You) (Paul)/
Some Other Guy/Thank You Girl/Sha La La La La! (Speech)/
Baby, It's You (John)/That's All Right (Mama) (Paul)/Carol (John)/
Soldier Of Love (John)/A Little Rhyme (Speech)/Clarabella (Paul/
I'm Gonna Sit Right Down And Cry (Over You)/Crying, Waiting, Hoping (George)/
Dear Wack! (Speech)/You Really Got A Hold On Me (John)/
To Know Her Is To Love Her (John)/ A Taste Of Honey (Paul)/
Long Tall Sally (Paul)/I Saw Her Standing There (Paul)/
The Honeymoon Song (Paul)/Johnny B. Goode (John)/
Memphis, Tennessee/Lucille (Paul)/
Can't Buy Me Love/From Fluff To You (Speech)/Till There Was You (Paul)

Disc Two:

Crinsk Dee Night (Speech)/A Hard Day's Night/Have A Banana! (Speech)/
I Wanna Be Your Man/Just A Rumour (Speech)/Roll Over Beethoven/
All My Loving/Things We said Today/
She's A Woman/Sweet Little Sixteen (John)/1822! (Speech)/
Lonesome Tears In My Eyes (John)/Nothin' Shakin' (George)/
The Hippy Hippy Shake (Paul)/Glad All Over (George)/I Just Don't Understand/
So How Come (No One Loves Me)/I Feel Fine/
I'm A Loser/Everybody's Trying To Be My Baby/Rock & Roll Music/
Ticket To Ride/Dizzy Miss Lizzy/Medley: Kansas City, Hey! Hey! Hey! Hey!/
Set Fire To That Lot (Speech)/Matchbox/I Forgot To Remember To Forget/
Love Those Goon Shows (Speech)/I Got To Find My Baby (John)/
Ooh! My Soul (Paul)/Ooh! My Arms (Speech)/Don't Ever Change (George)/
Slow Down/Honey Don't/Love Me Do

Baby It's You/I'll Follow The Sun/Devil In Her Heart/Boys

APPLE CDR 6406
RELEASED: MARCH 20 1995

1995.

'Anthology I'

APPLE 7243 8 34445 2 5
RELEASED: NOVEMBER 1995

Disc One:

Free As A Bird (John)/We Were Four Guys... (Speech)/That'll Be The Day/
In Spite Of All The Danger/Sometimes I'd Borrow... (Speech)/
Hallelujah, I Love Her So/You'll Be Mine (John)/Cayenne (Paul)/
First Of All... (Speech)/My Bonnie/Ain't She Sweet (John)/Cry For A Shadow/
Brian Was A Beautiful Guy... (Speech)/I Secured Them... (Speech)/Searchin'/
Three Cool Cats (George)/The Sheik Of Araby/Like Dreamers Do (Paul)/
Hello Little Girl (John)/Well, The Recording Test... (Speech)/Besame Mucho/
Love Me Do/How Do You Do It (John)/Please Please Me/One After 909/
Lend Me Your Comb/I'll Get You/We Were Performers... (Speech)/
I Saw Her Standing There/From Me To You/Money (That's What I Want)/
You Really Got A Hold On Me/Roll Over Beethoven

Disc Two:

She Loves You/Till There Was You/Twist And Shout/This Boy/
I Want To Hold Your Hand/Boys, What I Was Thinking... (Speech)/
Moonlight Bay/Can't Buy Me Love/All My Loving/You Can't Do That/
And I Love Her/A Hard Day's Night/I Wanna Be Your Man/
Long Tall Sally/Boys/Shout/I'll Be Back/
You Know What To Do (George)/ No Reply/Mr Moonlight/
Leave My Kitten Alone (John)/
No Reply/Eight Days A Week/Kansas City, Hey! Hey! Hey! Hey!/
Free As A Bird/I Saw Her Standing There/This Boy/
Christmas Time (Is Here Again)

1996.

'Anthology II'

APPLE 7243 8 3 4448 23
RELEASED: MARCH 1996

Disc One:

Real Love (John)/Yes It Is/I'm Down/You've Got To Hide Your Love Away/
If You've Got Trouble/That Means A Lot/Yesterday/It's Only Love/I Feel Fine/
Ticket To Ride/Yesterday/Help!/Everybody's Trying To Be My Baby/
Norwegian Wood (This Bird Has Flown)/I'm Looking Through You/

12-Bar Original/Tomorrow Never Knows/Got To Get You Into My Life/
And Your Bird Can Sing/Taxman/Eleanor Rigby/I'm Only Sleeping/
Rock & Roll Music/She's A Woman

Disc Two:
Strawberry Fields Forever/Penny Lane/A Day In The Life/
Good Morning, Good Morning/Only A Northern Song/
Being For The Benefit Of Mr Kite/Lucy In The Sky With Diamonds/
Within You, Without You/Sgt. Pepper's Lonely Hearts Club Band (Reprise)/
You Know My Name (Look Up The Number)/I Am The Walrus/The Fool On The Hill/Your
Mother Should Know/The Fool On The Hill/Hello, Goodbye/
Lady Madonna/Across The Universe

Real Love/Baby's In Black/Yellow Submarine/
Here, There & Everywhere

APPLE CDR 6425
RELEASED MARCH 1996

'Anthology III'
APPLE 7243 8 34451 27
RELEASED: OCTOBER 1996

Disc One:
A Beginning/Happiness Is A Warm Gun/Helter Skelter/Mean Mr Mustard/
Polythene Pam/Glass Onion/Junk/Piggies/Honey Pie/Don't Pass Me By/
Ob-La-Di, Ob-La-Da/Good Night/Cry Baby/Blackbird/
Sexy Sadie/While My Guitar Gently Weeps/Hey Jude/Not Guilty/
Mother Nature's Son/Glass Onion/Rocky Racoon/What's The New Mary Jane
(John and George, with Yoko)/Step Inside Love/Los Paranoias/
I'm So Tired/I Will/Why Don't We Do It In The Road/Julia

Disc Two:
I've Got A Feeling/She Came In Through The Bathroom Window/
Dig A Pony/Two Of Us/For You Blue/Teddy Boy (Paul)/
Medley: Rip It Up; Shake, Rattle & Roll; Blue Suede Shoes/
The Long And Winding Road/Oh! Darling/All Things Must Pass (George)/
Mailman, Bring Me No More Blues (John)/Get Back/Old Brown Shoe/
Octopus's Garden/Maxwell's Silver Hammer/Something/Come Together/
Come And Get It/Ain't She Sweet (John)/Because/Let It Be/I Me Mine/The End

Lyrics

Love Me Do

Love, love me do,
You know I love you.
I'll always be true,
So please
Love me do, woh love me do.

Love, love me do,
You know I love you.
I'll always be true,
So please
Love me do, woh love me do.

Someone to love, somebody new.
Someone to love, someone like you.

Love, love me do,
You know I love you.
I'll always be true,
So please
Love me do, woh love me do.

Love, love me do,
You know I love you.
I'll always be true,
So please
Love me do, woh love me do,
Yeah love me do, woh love me do.

P.S. I Love You

As I write this letter, send my love to you,
Remember that I'll always be in love with you.

Treasure these few words till we're together,
Keep all my love forever,
P.S. I love you,
You, you, you.

I'll be coming home again to you love,
Until the day I do love,
P.S. I love you,
You, you, you.

As I write this letter, send my love to you,
Remember that I'll always be in love with you.

Treasure these few words till we're together,
Keep all my love forever,
P.S. I love you,
You, you, you.

As I write this letter (Oh)
Send my love to you
You know I want you to
Remember that I'll always be in love with you.

I'll be coming home again to you love,
Until the day I do love,
P.S. I love you,
You, you, you.
You, you, you.
I love you.

Please Please Me

Last night I said these words to my girl,
I know you never even try, girl.

Come on, come on, come on, come on,
Please please me, woh yeah, like I please you.

You don't need me to show the way, love,
Why do I always have to say, love,

Come on, come on, come on, come on,
Please please me, woh yeah, like I please you.

I don't want to sound complaining,
But you know there's always rain in my heart.
I do all the pleasing with you,
It's so hard to reason with you,
Oh yeah, why do you make me blue?

Last night I said these words to my girl,
I know you never even try, girl.

Come on, come on, come on, come on,
Please please me, woh yeah, like I please you,
Please please me, woh yeah, like I please you
Please please me, woh yeah, like I please you.

Ask Me Why

I love you,
'Cause you tell me things I want to know.
And it's true that it really only goes to show
That I know
That I should never, never, never be blue.

Now you're mine,
My happiness still makes me cry.
And in time you'll understand the reason why
If I cry
It's not because I'm sad,
But you're the only love that I've ever had.

I can't believe it's happened to me.
I can't conceive of any more misery.

Ask me why,
I'll say I love you
And I'm always thinking of you.

I love you,
'Cause you tell me things I want to know.
And it's true that it really only goes to show
That I know
That I should never, never, never be blue.

Ask me why,
I'll say I love you,
And I'm always thinking of you,
You,
You.

From Me To You

If there's anything that you want,
If there's anything I can do,
Just call on me and I'll send it along,
With love from me to you.

I've got everything that you want,
Like a heart that's oh so true,
Just call on me and I'll send it along,
With love from me to you.

I got arms that long to hold you,
And keep you by my side.
I got lips that long to kiss you,
And keep you satisfied.

If there's anything that you want,
If there's anything I can do,
Just call on me and I'll send it along,
With love from me to you.

From me... to you.
Just call on me and I'll send it along,
With love from me to you.

I got arms that long to hold you,
And keep you by my side,
I got lips that long to kiss you,
And keep you satisfied.

If there's anything that you want,
If there's anything I can do,
Just call on me and I'll send it along
With love from me to you,
To you,
To you,
To you.

Thank You Girl

Oh, oh,
You've been good to me,
You made me glad when I was blue.
And eternally, I'll always be in love with you.

And all I gotta do is thank you girl,
Thank you girl.

I could tell the world
A thing or two about our love.
I know little girl,
Only a fool would doubt our love.

And all I gotta do is thank you girl,
Thank you girl.

Thank you girl for loving me the way that you do,
(Way that you do)
That's the kind of love that is too good to be true.
And all I gotta do is thank you girl,
Thank you girl.

Oh, oh,
You've been good to me,
You made me glad when I was blue.
And eternally I'll always be in love with you.
And all I gotta do is thank you girl,
Thank you girl.

Oh, oh, oh!
Oh, oh!

I Saw Her Standing There

Well, she was just seventeen,
You know what I mean,
And the way she looked was way beyond compare.
So how could I dance with another,
Oh, when I saw her standing there.

Well, she looked at me,
And I, I could see,
That before too long, I'd fall in love with her.
She wouldn't dance with another,
Oh, when I saw her standing there.

Well, my heart went boom
When I crossed that room,
And I held her hand in mine.

Well, we danced through the night,
And we held each other tight,
And before too long I fell in love with her.
Now I'll never dance with another,
Oh, when I saw her standing there.

Well, my heart went boom
When I crossed that room,
And I held her hand in mine.

Oh, we danced through the night,
And we held each other tight,
And before too long I fell in love with her,
Now I'll never dance with another,
Oh, since I saw her standing there,
Oh, since I saw her standing there,
Oh, since I saw her standing there.

Misery

The world is treating me bad, misery.

I'm the kind of guy who never used to cry,
The world is treating me bad, misery.

I've lost her now for sure,
I won't see her no more,
It's gonna be a drag, misery.

I'll remember all the little things we've done,
Can't she see she'll always be the only one, only one.

Send her back to me, 'cause everyone can see,
Without her I will be in misery.

I'll remember all the little things we've done,
She'll remember and she'll miss her only one, lonely one.

Send her back to me, 'cause everyone can see,
Without her I will be in misery.
Misery.
Oh, in misery. Oh, in misery,
La, la, la, la, la, la misery.

Do You Want To Know A Secret?

You'll never know how much I really love you,
You'll never know how much I really care.

Listen, do you want to know a secret?
Do you promise not to tell? Woh-woh.
Closer, let me whisper in your ear,
Say the words you long to hear,
I'm in love with you, ooh.

I've known the secret for a week or two,
Nobody knows, just we two.

Listen, do you want to know a secret?
Do you promise not to tell? Woh-woh.
Closer, let me whisper in your ear,
Say the words you long to hear,
I'm in love with you, ooh.
Ooh, ooh.

There's A Place

There,
There's a place where I can go,
When I feel low, when I feel blue.
And it's my mind, and there's no time
When I'm alone.

I,
I think of you and things you do
Go round my head, the things you've said,
Like, I love only you.

In my mind there's no sorrow,
Don't you know that it's so?
There'll be no sad tomorrow,
Don't you know that it's so?

There,
There's a place where I can go,
When I feel low, when I feel blue.
And it's my mind, and there's no time
When I'm alone.

There's a place,
There's a place,
There's a place,
There's a place.

She Loves You

She loves you, yeah, yeah, yeah,
She loves you yeah, yeah, yeah,
She loves you yeah, yeah, yeah, yeah.

You think you've lost your love,
Well I saw her yesterday.
It's you she's thinking of,
And she told me what to say.

She says she loves you,
And you know that can't be bad,
Yes, she loves you,
And you know you should be glad.

She said you hurt her so
She almost lost her mind,
But now she says she knows
You're not the hurting kind.

She says she loves you,
And you know that can't be bad,
Yes, she loves you,
And you know you should be glad.
(Ooh)

She loves you yeah, yeah, yeah,
She loves you yeah, yeah, yeah
And with a love like that,
You know you should be glad.

You know it's up to you,
I think it's only fair,
Pride can hurt you too,
Apologise to her.

Because she loves you,
And you know that can't be bad.
She loves you,
And you know you should be glad.
(Ooh)

She loves you, yeah, yeah, yeah,

She loves you, yeah, yeah, yeah
And with a love like that,
You know you should be glad.
With a love like that,
You know you should be glad.
With a love like that,
You know you should be glad.
Yeah, yeah, yeah,
Yeah, yeah, yeah, yeah.

I'll Get You

Oh yeah, oh yeah,
Oh yeah, oh yeah.

Imagine I'm in love with you,
It's easy 'cause I know
I've imagined I'm in love with you
Many, many, many times before.

It's not like me to pretend,
But I'll get you, I'll get you in the end,
Yes I will, I'll get you in the end,
Oh yeah, oh yeah.

I think about you night and day,
I need you and it's true,
When I think about you, I can say,
I'm never, never, never, never blue.

So I'm telling you, my friend,
That I'll get you, I'll get you in the end,
Yes I will, I'll get you in the end,
Oh yeah, oh yeah.

Well there's gonna be a time,
When I'm gonna change your mind.
So you might as well resign yourself to me,
Oh yeah.

Imagine I'm in love with you,
It's easy 'cause I know
I've imagined I'm in love with you,
Many, many, many times before.

It's not like me to pretend,
But I'll get you, I'll get you in the end,
Yes I will, I'll get you in the end,
Oh yeah, oh yeah,
Oh yeah, oh yeah, oh yeah.

I Want To Hold Your Hand

Oh yeah, I'll tell you something,
I think you'll understand,
Then I'll say that something,
I wanna hold your hand.

I wanna hold your hand,
I wanna hold your hand.

Oh please say to me
You'll let me be your man.
And please say to me
You'll let me hold your hand.

Now let me hold your hand,
I wanna hold your hand.

And when I touch you,
I feel happy inside,
It's such a feeling
That my love I can't hide,
I can't hide, I can't hide.

Yeah, you got that something,
I think you understand,
When I feel that something,
I wanna hold your hand.

I wanna hold your hand,
I wanna hold your hand,
I wanna hold your hand.

This Boy

That boy took my love away,
He'll regret it someday,
But this boy wants you back again.

That boy isn't good for you,
Though he may want you too,
This boy want you back again.

Oh, and this boy would be happy,
Just to love you, but oh my –
That boy won't be happy
Till he's seen you cry.

This boy wouldn't mind the pain,
Would always feel the same
If this boy gets you back again.

This boy,
This boy,
This boy.

It Won't Be Long

It won't be long, yeah, yeah, yeah,
It won't be long, yeah, yeah, yeah,
It won't be long, yeah,
Till I belong to you.

Every night when everybody has fun,
Here am I sitting all on my own.

It won't be long, yeah, yeah, yeah,
It won't be long, yeah, yeah, yeah,
It won't be long, yeah,
Till I belong to you.

Since you left me I'm so alone,
Now you're coming, you're coming on home,
I'll be good like I know I should
You're coming home, you're coming home.

Every night the tears come down from my eyes,
Every day I've done nothing but cry.
It won't be long, yeah, yeah, yeah,
It won't be long, yeah, yeah, yeah,
It won't be long, yeah,
Till I belong to you.

Since you left me I'm so alone,
Now you're coming, you're coming on home,
I'll be good like I know I should
You're coming home, you're coming home.

So, every day we'll be happy I know,
Now I know that you won't leave me no more.

It won't be long, yeah, yeah, yeah,
It won't be long, yeah, yeah, yeah,
It won't be long, yeah,
Till I belong to you.

All I've Got To Do

Whenever I want you around, yeah,
All I gotta do
Is call you on the phone
And you'll come running home,
Yeah, that's all I gotta do.

And when I wanna kiss you, yeah,
All I gotta do
Is whisper in your ear the words you long to hear,
And I'll be kissing you.

And the same goes for me, whenever you want me at all,
I'll be here, yes I will, whenever you call,
You just gotta call on me, yeah,
You just gotta call on me.

And when I wanna kiss you, yeah,
All I gotta do
Is call you on the phone
And you'll come running home,
Yeah, that's all I gotta do.

And the same goes for me, whenever you want me at all,
I'll be here, yes I will, whenever you call,
You just gotta call on me, yeah,
You just gotta call on me,
Oh, you just gotta call on me.
Mm, mm, mm, mm.

All My Loving

Close your eyes and I'll kiss you,
Tomorrow I'll miss you,
Remember, I'll always be true.
And then while I'm away,
I'll write home every day,
And I'll send all my loving to you.

I'll pretend that I'm kissing
The lips I am missing
And hope that my dreams will come true.
And then while I'm away,
I'll write home every day,
And I'll send all my loving to you.

All my loving I will send to you,
All my loving, darling I'll be true.

Close your eyes and I'll kiss you,
Tomorrow I'll miss you,
Remember I'll always be true.
And then while I'm away,
I'll write home every day,
And I'll send all my loving to you.

All my loving I will send to you,
All my loving, darling I'll be true.
All my loving, all my loving ooh,
All my loving I will send to you.

Don't Bother Me

Since she's been gone, I want no one to talk to me.
It's not the same, but I'm to blame, it's plain to see.
So go away, leave me alone, don't bother me.

I can't believe that she would leave me on my own.
It's just not right when every night I'm all alone.
I've got no time for you right now, don't bother me.

I know I'll never be the same
If I don't get her back again,
Because I know she'll always be
The only girl for me.

But till she's here please don't come near, just stay away.
I'll let you know when she's come home – until that day,
Don't come around, leave me alone, don't bother me.
I've got no time for you right now, don't bother me.

I know I'll never be the same
If I don't get her back again,
Because I know she'll always be
The only girl for me.

But till she's here, please don't come near, just stay away.
I'll let you know when she's come home – until that day
Don't come around, leave me alone, don't bother me.
Don't bother me, don't bother me, don't bother me.

Little Child

Little child, little child,
Little child, won't you dance with me?
I'm so sad and lonely,
Baby take a chance with me.

Little child, little child,
Little child, won't you dance with me?
I'm so sad and lonely,
Baby take a chance with me.

If you want someone to make you feel so fine,
Then we'll have some fun when you're mine, all mine,
So come on, come on, come on!

Little child, little child,
Little child, won't you dance with me?
I'm so sad and lonely,
Baby take a chance with me.

When you're by my side, you're the only one,
Don't you run and hide, just come on, come on,
Yeah, come on, come on, come on!

Little child, little child,
Little child, won't you dance with me?
I'm so sad and lonely,
Baby take a chance with me,
Oh yeah, baby take a chance with me,
Oh yeah, baby take a chance with me.

Hold Me Tight

It feel so right now, hold me tight,
Tell me I'm the only one,
And then I might
Never be the lonely one.

So hold me tight, tonight, tonight,
It's you,
You, you, you.

Hold me tight,
Let me go on loving you.
Tonight, tonight,
Making love to only you.

So hold me tight, tonight, tonight,
It's you,
You, you, you.

Don't know what it means to hold you tight,
Being here alone tonight with you,
It feels so right now.

Hold me tight,
Tell me I'm the only one,
And then I might
Never be the lonely one.

So hold me tight, tonight, tonight,
It's you,
You, you, you.

Don't know what it means to hold you tight,
Being here alone tonight with you,
It feels so right now.

Hold me tight,
Let me go on loving you.
Tonight, tonight,
Making love to only you.

So hold me tight, tonight, tonight,
It's you,
You, you, you,
You.

I Wanna Be Your Man

I wanna be your lover, baby,
I wanna be your man,
I wanna be your lover, baby,
I wanna be your man.

Love you like no other, baby,
Like no other can,
Love you like no other, baby,
Like no other can.

I wanna be your man,
I wanna be your man,
I wanna be your man,
I wanna be your man.

Tell me that you love me, baby,
Let me understand,
Tell me that you love me, baby,
I wanna be your man.

I wanna be your lover, baby,
I wanna be your man,
I wanna be your lover, baby,
I wanna be your man.

I wanna be your man,
I wanna be your man,
I wanna be your man,
I wanna be your man.

I wanna be your lover, baby,
I wanna be your man,
I wanna be your lover, baby,
I wanna be your man.

Love you like no other, baby,
Like no other can,
Love you like no other, baby,
Like no other can.

I wanna be your man,
I wanna be your man,
I wanna be your man,
I wanna be your man...

Not A Second Time

You know you made me cry,
I see no use in wondering why,
I cried for you.

And now you've changed your mind,
I see no reason to change mine,
My crying is through, oh.

You're giving me the same old line,
I'm wondering why.
You hurt me then, you're back again,
No, no, no, not a second time.

You know you made me cry,
I see no use in wondering shy,
I cried for you, yeah.

And now you've changed your mind,
I see no reason to change mine,
My crying is through, oh.

You're giving me the same old line,
I'm wondering why.
You hurt me then, you're back again,
No, no, no, not a second time.

Not a second time.
Not a second time...

Can't Buy Me Love

Can't buy me love, love,
Can't buy me love.

I'll buy you a diamond ring my friend,
If it makes you feel alright.
I'll get you anything my friend,
If it makes you feel alright.
'Cause I don't care too much for money,
Money can't buy me love.

I'll give you all I've got to give,
If you say you love me too.
I may not have a lot to give,
But what I've got I'll give to you.
I don't care too much for money,
Money can't buy me love.

Can't buy me love, everybody tells me so.
Can't buy me love, no, no, no, no.

Say you don't need no diamond rings
And I'll be satisfied.
Tell me that you want the kind of things
That money just can't buy.
I don't care too much for money,
Money can't buy me love.

Can't buy me love, everybody tells me so,
Can't buy me love, no, no, no, no.

Say you don't need no diamond rings
And I'll be satisfied.
Tell me that you want the kind of things
That money just can't buy.
I don't care too much for money,
Money can't buy me love.

Can't buy me love, love,
Can't buy me love.

You Can't Do That

I got something to say that might cause you pain,
If I catch you talking to that boy again,
I'm gonna let you down
And leave you flat.
Because I told you before,
Oh, you can't do that.

Well, it's the second time I've caught you talking to him,
Do I have to tell you one more time, I think it's a sin.
I think I'll let you down (Let you down)
And leave you flat
(Gonna let you down and leave you flat).
Because I've told you before,
Oh, you can't do that.

Everybody's green
'Cause I'm the one who won your love.
But if they'd seen
You talking that way,
They'd laugh in my face.

So please listen to me if you wanna stay mine,
I can't help my feelings, I'll go out of my mind,
I'm gonna let you down (Let you down)
And leave you flat
(Gonna let you down and leave you flat).
Because I've told you before,
Oh, you can't do that.

Everybody's green
'Cause I'm the one who won your love.
But if they'd seen
You talking that way
They'd laugh in my face.

So please listen to me, if you wanna stay mine,
I can't help my feelings, I'll go out of my mind,
I'll go and let you down (Let you down)
And leave you flat
(Gonna let you down and leave you flat).
Because I've told you before,
Oh, you can't do that.

I Call Your Name

I call your name, but you're not there.
Was I to blame for being unfair?
Oh, I can't sleep at night since you've been gone.
I never weep at night, I can't go on.

Don't you know I can't take it?
I don't know who can.
I'm not goin' to make it,
I'm not that kind of man.

Oh, I can't sleep at night, but just the same,
I never weep at night, I call your name.

Don't you know I can't take it?
I don't know who can.
I'm not goin' to make it,
I'm not that kind of man.

Oh, I can't sleep at night, but just the same,
I never weep at night, I call your name,
I call your name,
I call your name...

A Hard Day's Night

It's been a hard day's night,
And I've been working like a dog.
It's been a hard day's night,
I should be sleeping like a log.
But when I get home to you,
I find the things that you do
Will make me feel alright.

You know, I work all day
To get you money, to buy you things.
And it's worth it just to hear you say
You're gonna give me everything.
So why on earth should I moan,
'Cause when I get you alone,
You know I feel okay.

When I'm home, everything seems to be right.
When I'm home, feeling you holding me
Tight, tight, yeah.

It's been a hard day's night,
And I've been working like a dog.
It's been a hard day's night,
I should be sleeping like a log.
But when I get home to you,
I find the things that you do
Will make me feel alright.

So why on earth should I moan,
'Cause when I get you alone,
You know I feel okay.

When I'm home, everything seems to be right.
When I'm home, feeling you holding me
Tight, tight yeah.

Ooh, it's been a hard day's night,
And I've been working like a dog.
It's been a hard day's night,
I should be sleeping like a log.
But when I get home to you,
I find the things that you do

Will make me feel alright.
You know I feel alright.
You know I feel alright.

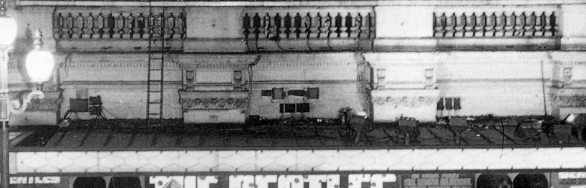

I Should Have Known Better

I should have known better with a girl like you,
That I would love everything that you do,
And I do, hey hey hey, and I do.

Woh woh, I never realised what a kiss could be,
This could only happen to me.
Can't you see, can't you see?

That when I tell you that I love you, oh,
You're gonna say you love me too.
Oh, and when I ask you to be mine.
You're gonna say you love me too.

So, oh, I should have realised a lot of things before.
If this is love, you've got to give me more,
Give me more, hey hey hey, give me more.

Woh woh, I never realised what a kiss could be,
This could only happen to me.
Can't you see, can't you see?

That when I tell you that I love you, oh,
You're gonna say you love me too,
Oh, and when I ask you to be mine,
You're gonna say you love me too.
You love me too.
You love me too.
You love me too.

If I Fell

If I fell in love with you,
Would you promise to be true
And help me understand?
'Cause I've been in love before,
And I found that love was more
Than just holding hands.

If I give my heart to you,
I must be sure from the very start
That you would love me more than her.

If I trust in you, oh please,
Don't run and hide.
If I love you too, oh please,
Don't hurt my pride like her.

'Cause I couldn't stand the pain,
And I would be sad if our new love
Was in vain.

So I hope you see
That I would love to love you,
And that she will cry
When she learns we are two.

'Cause I couldn't stand the pain
And I would be sad if our new love
Was in vain.

So I hope you see
That I would love to love you,
And that she will cry when she learns we are two.
If I fell in love with you.

I'm Happy Just To Dance With You

Before this dance is through
I think I'll love you too,
I'm so happy when you dance with me.

I don't wanna kiss or hold your hand,
If it's funny, try and understand.
There is really nothing else I'd rather do,
'Cause I'm happy just to dance with you.

I don't need to hug or hold you tight,
I just wanna dance with you all night.
In this world there's nothing I would rather do,
'Cause I'm happy just to dance with you.

Just to dance with you is everything I need.
Before this dance is through
I think I'll love you too,
I'm so happy when you dance with me.

If somebody tries to take my place,
Let's pretend we just can't see his face.
In this world there's nothing I would rather do,
'Cause I'm happy just to dance with you.

Just to dance with you is everything I need.
Before this dance is through,
I think I'll love you too,
I'm so happy when you dance with me.

If somebody tries to take my place,
Let's pretend we just can't see his face.
In this world there's nothing I would rather do,
I've discovered I'm in love with you.
'Cause I'm happy just to dance with you.

And I Love Her

I give her all my love,
That's all I do,
And if you saw my love,
You'd love her too,
And I love her.

She gives me everything,
And tenderly,
The kiss my lover brings,
She brings to me,
And I love her.

A love like ours
Could never die
As long as I
Have you near me.

Bright are the stars that shine,
Dark is the sky,
I know this love of mine,
Will never die
And I love her.

Bright are the stars that shine,
Dark is the sky.
I know this love of mine.
Will never die
And I love her.

Tell Me Why

Tell me why you cried,
And why you lied to me.
Tell me why you cried,
And why you lied to me.

Well I gave you everything I had,
But you left me sitting on my own.
Did you have to treat me oh so bad?
All I do is hang my head and moan.

Tell me why you cried,
And why you lied to me.
Tell me why you cried,
And why you lied to me.

If it's something that I've said or done,
Tell me what and I'll apologise.
If you don't, I really can't go on,
Holding back these tears in my eyes.

Tell me why you cried,
And why you lied to me.
Tell me why you cried,
And why you lied to me.

Well I beg you on my bended knees,
If you'll only listen to my pleas,
Is there anything I can do?
'Cause I really can't stand it,
I'm so in love with you.

Tell me why you cried,
And why you lied to me.
Tell me why you cried,
And why you lied to me.

Any Time At All

Any time at all,
Any time at all,
Any time at all,
All you've gotta do is call
And I'll be there.

If you need somebody to love,
Just look into my eyes,
I'll be there to make you feel right.

If you're feeling sorry and sad,
I'd really sympathise.
Don't you be sad, just call me tonight.

Any time at all,
Any time at all,
Any time at all,
All you've gotta do is call,
And I'll be there.

If the sun has faded away,
I'll try to make it shine.
There is nothing I won't do.

When you need a shoulder to cry on,
I hope it will be mine.
Call me tonight, and I'll come to you.

Any time at all,
Any time at all,
Any time at all,
All you've gotta do is call
And I'll be there.

Any time at all,
Any time at all,
Any time at all,
All you've gotta do is call
And I'll be there.
Any time at all,
All you've gotta do is call
And I'll be there.

I'll Cry Instead

I've got every reason on earth to be mad,
'Cause I've just lost the only girl I had.
And if I could get my way,
I'd get myself locked up today,
But I can't, so I'll cry instead.

I've got a chip on my shoulder that's bigger than my feet.
I can't talk to people that I meet.
If I could see you now,
I'd try to make you sad somehow,
But I can't, so I'll cry instead.

Don't want to cry when there's people there,
I get shy when they start to stare.
I'm gonna lock myself away,
But I'll come back again some day.

And when I do, you better hide all the girls,
I'm gonna break their hearts all round the world.
Yes, I'm gonna break them in two,
Show you what your lovin' man can do,
Until then I'll cry instead.

Don't want to cry when there's people there,
I get shy when they start to stare.
I'm gonna hide myself away,
But I'll come back again some day.

And when I do you'd better hide all the girls,
'Cause I'm gonna break their hearts all round the world.
Yes, I'm gonna break them in two
And show you what your lovin' man can do,
Until then I'll cry instead.

Things We Said Today

You say you will love me if I have to go,
You'll be thinking of me, somehow I will know.
Someday when I'm lonely,
Wishing you weren't so far away,
Then I will remember things we said today.

You say you'll be mine, girl, till the end of time,
These days, such a kind girl seems so hard to find.
Someday when we're dreaming,
Deep in love, not a lot to say,
Then we will remember things we said today.

Me, I'm just the lucky kind,
Love to hear you say that love is love,
And though we may be blind,
Love is here to stay
And that's enough

To make you mine, girl,
Be the only one.
Love me all the time, girl,
We'll go on and on.
Someday when we're dreaming,
Deep in love, not a lot to say,
Then we will remember things we said today.

Me, I'm just the lucky kind
Love to hear you say that love is love,
And though we may be blind,
Love is here to stay
And that's enough

To make you mine, girl,
Be the only one.
Love me all the time, girl, we'll go on and on.
Someday when we're dreaming,
Deep in love, not a lot to say,
Then we will remember things we said today.

When I Get Home

Woh-ah, woh-ah,
I got a whole lot of things to tell her
When I get home.

Come on, out my way,
'Cause I'm a-gonna see my baby today,
I've got a whole lot of things I've gotta say to her.
Woh-ah, Woh-ah,
I got a whole lot of things to tell her,
When I get home.

Come on if you please,
I've got not time for triviality,
I've got a girl who's waiting home for me tonight.
Woh-ah, woh-ah,
I got a whole lot of things to tell her,
When I get home.

When I'm getting home tonight,
I'm gonna hold her tight,
I'm gonna love her till the cows come home
I bet I'll love her more,
Till I walk out that door – again.

Come on, let me through,
I've got so many things I've got to do,
I've got no business being here with you this way.
Woh-ah, woh-ah,
I got a whole lot of things to tell her,
When I get home – yeah.
I've got a whole lot of things to tell her
When I get home.

I'll Be Back

You know if you break my heart I'll go,
But I'll be back again.
'Cause I told you once before goodbye,
But I came back again.

I love you so,
I'm the one who wants you,
Yes I'm the one who wants you,
Oh-ho, oh-ho.

You could find better things to do,
Than to break my heart again.
This time I will try to show that I'm
Not trying to pretend.

I thought that you would realise,
That if I ran away from you,
That you would want me too,
But I got a big surprise, oh-ho, oh-ho.

You could find better things to do
Than to break my heart again.
This time I will try to show that I'm
Not trying to pretend.

I wanna go,
But I hate to leave you,
You know I hate to leave you,
Oh-ho, oh-ho.

You, if you break my heart I'll go,
But I'll be back again.

I Feel Fine

Baby's good to me you know,
She's happy as can be, you know
She said so.
I'm in love with her and I feel fine.

Baby says she's mine you know,
She tells me all the time, you know
She said so.
I'm in love with her and I feel fine.

I'm so glad that she's my little girl,
She's so glad, she's telling all the world

That her baby buys her things you know,
He buys her diamond rings, you know
She said so.
She's in love with me and I feel fine.

Baby says she's mine you know,
She tells me all the time, you know
She said so.
I'm in love with her and I feel fine.

I'm so glad that she's my little girl,
She's so glad, she's telling all the world

That her baby buys her things you know,
He buys her diamond rings, you know
She said so.
She's in love with me and I feel fine.
She's in love with me and I feel fine.

She's A Woman

My love don't give me presents,
I know that she's no peasant.
Only ever has to give me
Love forever and forever,
My love don't give me presents.
Turn me on when I get lonely,
People tell me that she's only foolin',
I know she isn't.

She don't give boys the eye.
She hate to see me cry.
She is happy just to hear me
Say that I will never leave her,
She don't give boys the eye.
She will never make me jealous,
Give me all her time as well as lovin',
Don't ask me why.

She's a woman who understands,
She's a woman who loves her man.

My love don't give me presents,
I know that she's no peasant.
Only ever has to give me
Love forever and forever,
My love don't give me presents.
Turn me on when I get lonely,
People tell me that she's only foolin',
I know she isn't.

She's a woman who understands,
She's a woman who loves her man.

My love don't give me presents,
I know that she's no peasant.
Only ever has to give me
Love forever and forever,
My love don't give me presents.
Turn me on when I get lonely,
People tell me that she's only foolin',
I know she isn't.

She's a woman, she's a woman,
She's a woman, she's a woman...

No Reply

This happened once before,
When I came to your door – no reply.
They said it wasn't you,
But I saw you peep through your window.

I saw the light, I saw the light.
I know that you saw me,
'Cause I looked up to see your face.

I tried to telephone,
They said you were not home – that's a lie.
'Cause I know where you've been,
I saw you walk in your door.

I nearly died, I nearly died,
'Cause you walked hand in hand
With another man in my place.

If I were you, I'd realise that I
Love you more than any other guy.
And I'll forgive the lies that I
Heard before, when you gave me no reply.

I tried to telephone,
They said you were not home – that's a lie.
'Cause I know where you've been,
And I saw you walk in your door.

I nearly died, I nearly died,
'Cause you walked hand in hand
With another man in my place.

No reply, no reply.

I'm A Loser

I'm a loser, I'm a loser,
And I'm not what I appear to be.

Of all the love I have won or have lost,
There is one love I should never have crossed.
She was a girl in a million my friend,
I should have known she would win in the end.

I'm a loser, and I lost someone who's near to me,
I'm a loser, and I'm not what I appear to be.

Although I laugh and I act like a clown,
Beneath this mask I am wearing a frown.
My tears are falling like rain from the sky,
Is it for her or myself that I cry?

I'm a loser, and I lost someone who's near to me,
I'm a loser, and I'm not what I appear to be.

What have I done to deserves such a fate?
I realise I have left it too late.
And so it's true, pride comes before a fall,
I'm telling you so that you won't lose all.

I'm a loser, and I lost someone who's near to me,
I'm a loser, and I'm not what I appear to be.

Baby's In Black

Oh dear, what can I do?
Baby's in black and I'm feeling blue,
Tell me, oh what can can I do?

She thinks of him,
And so she dresses in black,
And though he'll never come back,
She's dressed in black.

Oh dear, what can I do?
Baby's in black and I'm feeling blue,
Tell me, oh what can I do?

I think of her,
But she thinks only of him,
And though it's only a whim,
She thinks of him.

Oh, how long will it take,
Till she sees the mistake she has made?
Dear, what can I do?
Baby's in black and I'm feeling blue,
Tell me, oh, what can I do?

Oh, how long will it take,
Till she sees the mistake she has made?
Dear, what can I do?
Baby's in black and I'm feeling blue,
Tell me, oh, what can I do?

She thinks of him,
And so she dresses in black,
And though he'll never come back,
She's dressed in black.

Oh dear, what can I do?
Baby's in black and I'm feeling blue
Tell me, oh, what can I do?

I'll Follow The Sun

Once day you'll look
To see I've gone,
For tomorrow may rain, so
I'll follow the sun.

Some day you'll know
I was the one,
But tomorrow may rain, so
I'll follow the sun.

And now the time has come
And so my love I must go.
And though I lose a friend,
In the end you will know, oh.

One day you'll find
That I have gone,
For tomorrow may rain, so
I'll follow the sun.

Yes, tomorrow may rain, so
I'll follow the sun.

And now the time has come
And so my love I must go.
And though I lose a friend,
In the end you will know, oh.

One day you'll find
That I have gone,
For tomorrow may rain, so
I'll follow the sun.

Eight Days A Week

Ooh I need your love, babe,
Guess you know it's true.
Hope you need my love, babe,
Just like I need you.

Hold me, love me,
Hold me, love me,
I ain't got nothin' but love, babe,
Eight days a week.

Love you every day, girl,
Always on my mind.
One thing I can say, girl,
Love you all the time.

Hold me, love me,
Hold me, love me,
I ain't got nothin' but love, girl,
Eight days a week.

Eight days a week I love you.
Eight days a week
Is not enough to show I care.

Ooh I need your love, babe,
Guess you know it's true.
Hope you need my love, babe,
Just like I need you.

Oh, hold me, love me,
Hold me, love me,
I ain't got nothin' but love, babe,
Eight days a week.

Eight days a week I love you.
Eight days a week
Is not enough to show I care.

Love you every day, girl,
Always on my mind.
One thing I can say, girl,
Love you all the time.

Hold me, love me,
Hold me, love me,
I ain't got nothin' but love, babe,
Eight days a week,
Eight days a week,
Eight days a week.

Every Little Thing

When I'm walking beside her,
People tell me I'm lucky,
Yes, I know I'm a lucky guy.

I remember the first time
I was lonely without her,
Yes, I'm thinking about her now.

Every little thing she does,
She does for me, yeah,
And you know the things she does,
She does for me, ooh.

When I'm with her I'm happy,
Just to know that she loves me,
Yes I know that she loves me now.

There is one thing I'm sure of,
I will love her forever,
For I know love will never die.

Every little thing she does,
She does for me, yeah,
And you know the things she does,
She does for me, ooh.

Every little thing she does,
She does for me, yeah,
And you know the things she does,
She does for me, ooh.
Every little thing.
Every little thing.

I Don't Want To Spoil The Party

I don't want to spoil the party so I'll go,
I would hate my disappointment to show.
There's nothing for me here, so I will disappear,
If she turns up while I'm gone, please let me know.

I've had a drink or two and I don't care,
There's no fun in what I do if she's not there.
I wonder what went wrong, I've waited far too long,
I think I'll take a walk and look for her.

Though tonight she's made me sad,
I still love her.
If I find her I'll be glad,
I still love her.

I don't want to spoil the party so I'll go,
I would hate my disappointment to show.
There's nothing for me here, so I will disappear,
If she turns up while I'm gone, please let me know.

Though tonight she's made me sad,
I still love her.
If I find her I'll be glad,
I still love her.

So, I've had a drink or two and I don't care,
There's no fun in what I do if she's not there.
I wonder what went wrong, I've waited far too long,
I think I'll take a walk and look for her.

What You're Doing

Look what you're doing,
I'm feeling blue and lonely,
Would it be too much to ask of you,
What you're doing to me?

You got me running
And there's no fun in it,
Why should it be so much to ask of you,
What you're doing to me?

I've been waiting here for you,
Wondering what you're gonna do,
And should you need a love that's true, it's me.

Please stop your lying,
You've got me crying, girl,
Why should it be so much to ask of you,
What you're doing to me?

I've been waiting here for you,
Wondering what you're gonna do
Should you need a love that's true, it's me.

Please stop your lying,
You've got me crying, girl,
Why should it be so much to ask of you
What you're doing to me?
What you're doing to me.
What you're doing to me.

Ticket To Ride

I think I'm gonna be sad,
I think it's today, yeah.
The girl that's driving me mad
Is going away, yeah.

She's got a ticket to ride,
She's got a ticket to ride,
She's got a ticket to ride, but she don't care.

She said that living with me,
Was bringing her down, yeah.
She would never be free,
When I was around.

She's got a ticket to ride,
She's got a ticket to ride,
She's got a ticket to ride, but she don't care.

I don't know shy she's riding so high,
She ought to think twice,
She ought to do right by me.
Before she gets to saying goodbye,
She ought to think twice,
She ought to do right by me.

I think I'm gonna be sad,
I think it's today, yeah,
The girl that's driving me mad,
Is going away, yeah.

Ah, she's got a ticket to ride,
She's got a ticket to ride,
She's got a ticket to ride, but she don't care.

I don't know why she's riding so high,
She ought to think twice,
She ought to do right by me.
Before she gets to saying goodbye,
She ought to think twice,
She ought to do right by me.

She said that living with me,

Was bringing her down, yeah.
She would never be free,
When I was around.

Ah, she's got a ticket to ride,
She's got a ticket to ride,
She's got a ticket to ride, but she don't care.

My baby don't care, my baby don't care,
My baby don't care, my baby don't care...

Yes It Is

If you wear red tonight,
Remember what I said tonight,
For red is the colour that my baby wore,
And what's more, it's true,
Yes it is.

Scarlet were the clothes she wore,
Everybody knows I'm sure,
I would remember all the things we planned,
Understand, it's true,
Yes it is, it's true,
Yes it is.

I could be happy with you by my side,
If I could forget her,
But it's my pride,
Yes it is, yes it is,
Oh yes it is, yeah.

Please don't wear red tonight,
This is what I said tonight,
For red is the colour that will make me blue,
In spite of you, it's true,
Yes it is, it's true,
Yes it is.

I could be happy with you by my side,
If I could forget her,
But it's my pride,
Yes it is, yes it is,
Oh yes it is, yeah.

Please don't wear red tonight,
This is what I said tonight,
For red is the colour that will make me blue,
In spite of you it's true,
Yes it is, it's true,
Yes it is, it's true.

Help!

Help! I need somebody,
Help! Not just anybody,
Help! You know I need someone,
Help!

When I was younger, so much younger than today,
I never needed anybody's help in any way.
But now these days are gone I'm not so self assured,
Now I find I've changed my mind and opened up the doors.

Help me if you can, I'm feeling down
And I do appreciate you being 'round,
Help me get my feet back on the ground,
Won't you please, please help me?

And now my life has changed in oh so many ways,
My independence seems to vanish in the haze.
But every now and then I feel so insecure,
I know that I just need you like I've never done before.

Help me if you can, I'm feeling down,
And I do appreciate you being 'round,
Help me get my feet back on the ground,
Won't you please, please help me?

When I was younger, so much younger than today,
I never needed anybody's help in any way.
But now these days are gone I'm not so self assured,
Now I find I've changed my mind and opened up the doors.

Help me if you can, I'm feeling down,
And I do appreciate you being 'round,
Help me get my feet back on the ground,
Won't you please, please help me,
Help me, help me – ooh.

I'm Down

You tell lies thinkin' I can't see,
You can't cry 'cause you're laughing at me,

I'm down (I'm really down),
I'm down (Down on the ground),
I'm down (I'm really down),
How can you laugh when you know I'm down?
(How can you laugh) When you know I'm down?

Man buys ring, woman throws it away,
Same old thing happens every day,
I'm down (I'm really down),
I'm down (Down on the ground),
I'm down (I'm really down),
How can you laugh when you know I'm down?
(How can you laugh)When you know I'm down?

We're all alone and there's nobody else,
You still moan, Keep your hands to yourself,

I'm down (I'm really down),
I'm down (Down on the ground),
I'm down (I'm really down),
How can you laugh when you know I'm down?
(How can you laugh) When you know I'm down?

Oh babe, you know I'm down (I'm really down)
Oh yes I'm down (I'm really down)
I'm down on the ground (I'm really down)
I'm down (I'm really down)
Ah, baby, I'm upside down
Oh yeah, yeah, yeah, yeah, yeah,
I'm down...

The Night Before

We said our goodbyes (Ah, the night before),
Love was in your eyes (Ah, the night before),
Now today I find, you have changed your mind,
Treat me like you did the night before.

Were you telling lies? (Ah, the night before)
Was I so unwise? (Ah, the night before)
When I held you near, you were so sincere,
Treat me like you did the night before.

Last night is the night I will remember you by,
When I think of things we did, it makes me wanna cry.

We said our goodbyes (Ah, the night before),
Love was in your eyes (Ah, the night before),
Now today I find, you have changed your mind,
Treat me like you did the night before.
Yes...

When I held you near, you were so sincere,
Treat me like you did the night before.

Last night is the night I will remember you by,
When I think of things we did, it makes me wanna cry.

Were you telling lies? (Ah, the night before)
Was I so unwise? (Ah, the night before)
When I held you near, you were so sincere,
Treat me like you did the night before,
Like the night before.

You've Got To Hide Your Love Away

Here I stand, head in hand,
Turn my face to the wall.
If she's gone, I can't go on,
Feeling two foot small.

Everywhere people stare,
Each and every day.
I can see them laugh at me,
And I hear them say:

Hey, you've got to hide your love away,
Hey, you've got to hide your love away.

How can I even try?
I can never win.
Hearing them, seeing them,
In the state I'm in.

How could she say to me
Love will find a way?
Gather round all you clowns
Let me hear you say:

Hey, you've got to hide your love away,
Hey, you've got to hide your love away.

I Need You

You don't realise how much I need you,
Love you all the time and never leave you.
Please come on back to me, I'm lonely as can be,
I need you.

Said you had a thing or two to tell me,
How was I to know you would upset me?
I didn't realise as I looked in your eyes,
You told me.

Oh yes you told me
You don't want my lovin' anymore.
That's when it hurt me, and feeling like this
I just can't go on anymore.

Please remember how I feel about you,
I could never really live without you.
So, come on back and see
Just what you mean to me,
I need you.

But when you told me
You don't want my lovin' anymore,
That's when it hurt me, and feeling like this
I just can't go on anymore.

Please remember how I feel about you,
I could never really live without you.
So come on back and see
Just what you mean to me,
I need you.
I need you.
I need you.

Another Girl

For I have got another girl, another girl.
You're making me say that I've got nobody but you,
But as from today, well I've got somebody that's new.
I ain't no fool and I don't take what I don't want,
For I have got another girl, another girl.

She's sweeter than all the girls and I've met quite a few.
Nobody in all the world can do what she can do.
And so I'm telling you this time you'd better stop,
For I have got another girl.

Another girl who will love me till the end,
Through thick and thin, she will always be my friend.

I don't wanna say that I've been unhappy with you,
But as from today, well I've seen somebody that's new.
I ain't no fool and I don't take what I don't want,
For I have got another girl.

Another girl who will love me till the end,
Through thick and thin she will always be my friend.

I don't wanna say that I've been unhappy with you,
But as from today, well I've seen somebody that's new.
I ain't no fool and I don't take what I don't want,
For I have got another girl,
Another girl, another girl.

You're Going To Lose That Girl

You're gonna lose that girl, you're gonna lose that girl.

If you don't take her out tonight, she's gonna change her mind,
And I will take her out tonight, and I will treat her kind.
You're gonna lose that girl, you're gonna lose that girl.

If you don't treat her right, my friend, you're gonna find her gone,
'Cause I will treat her right and then you'll be the lonely one.
You're gonna lose that girl, you're gonna lose that girl,
You're gonna lose...

I'll make a point of taking her away from you, yeah.
The way you treat her, what else can I do?

You're gonna lose that girl, you're gonna lose that girl,
You're gonna lose...

I'll make a point of taking her away from you, yeah.
The way you treat her, what else can I do?

If you don't take her out tonight, she's going to change her mind,
And I will take her out tonight, and I will treat her kind.
You're gonna lose that girl, you're gonna lose that girl,
You're gonna lose that girl.

It's Only Love

I get high when I see you go by,
My oh my,
When you sigh my, my inside just flies,
Butterflies.
Why am I so shy when I'm beside you?

It's only love and that is all,
Why should I feel the way I do?
It's only love and that is all,
But it's so hard loving you.

Is it right that you and I should fight
Every night?
Just the sight of you makes night time bright,
Very bright.
Haven't I the right to make it up, girl?

It's only love and that is all,
Why should I feel the way I do?
It's only love and that is all,
But it's so hard loving you,
Yes it's so hard loving you,
Loving you.

You Like Me Too Much

Though you've gone away this morning,
You'll be back again tonight,
Telling me there'll be no next time
If I just don't treat you right.

You'll never leave me and you know it's true,
'Cause you like me too much and I like you.

You've tried before to leave me,
But you haven't had the nerve,
To walk out and make me lonely,
Which is all that I deserve.

You'll never leave me and you know it's true,
'Cause you like me too much and I like you.

I really do,
And it's nice when you believe me.
If you leave me,

I will follow you and bring you
Back where you belong,
'Cause I couldn't really stand it,
I'd admit that I was wrong.

I wouldn't let you leave me, 'cause it's true,
'Cause you like me too much and I like you.

I really do,
And it's nice when you believe me.
If you leave me,

I will follow you
And bring you back where you belong,
'Cause I couldn't really stand it,
I'd admit that I was wrong.

I wouldn't let you leave me, 'cause it's true,
'Cause you like me too much and I like you,
'Cause you like me too much and I like you.

Tell Me What You See

If you let me take your heart,
I will prove to you,
We will never be apart
If I'm part of you.

Open up your eyes now,
Tell me what you see,
It is no surprise now,
What you see is me.

Big and black the clouds may be,
Time will pass away,
If you put your trust in me,
I'll make bright your day.

Look into these eyes now,
Tell me what you see,
Don't you realise now,
What you see is me?
Tell me what you see.

Listen to me one more time,
How can I get through?
Can't you try to see that I'm
Trying to get to you?

Open up your eyes now,
Tell me what you see,
It is no surprise now,
What you see is me.
Tell me what you see.

Listen to me one more time,
How can I get through?
Can't you try to see that I'm
Trying to get to you?

Open up your eyes now,
Tell me what you see,
It is no surprise now,
What you see is me.
Mmm-mmm.

I've Just Seen A Face

I've just seen a face,
I can't forget the time or place where we just met,
She's just the girl for me
And I want all the world to see we've met.
Mm mm mm mm-mm mm.

Had it been another day
I might have looked the other way
And I'd have never been aware,
But as it is I'll dream of her tonight,
Da da da da-da da.

Falling, yes I am falling,
And she keeps calling me back again.

I have never known the like of this,
I've been alone and I have
Missed things and kept out of sight,
For other girls were never quite like this,
Da da da da-da da.

Falling, yes I am falling,
And she keeps calling me back again.
Falling, yes I am falling,
And she keeps calling me back again.

I've just seen a face,
I can't forget the time or place where we just met,
She's just the girl for me
And I want all the world to see we've met,
Mm mm mm, da-da da.

Falling, yes I am falling,
And she keeps calling me back again.
Falling, yes I am falling,
And she keeps calling me back again.
Oh, falling, yes I am falling,
And she keeps calling me back again.

Yesterday

Yesterday, all my troubles seemed so far away,
Now it looks as though they're here to stay,
Oh I believe in yesterday.

Suddenly, I'm not half the man I used to be,
There's a shadow hanging over me,
Oh yesterday came suddenly.

Why she had to go, I don't know, she wouldn't say.
I said something wrong, now I long for yesterday.

Yesterday, love was such an easy game to play,
Now I need a place to hide away,
Oh I believe in yesterday.

Why she had to go, I don't know, she wouldn't say.
I said something wrong, now I long for yesterday.

Yesterday, love was such an easy game to play,
Now I need a place to hide away,
Oh I believe in yesterday.
Mm mm mm mm mm mm-mm.

Drive My Car

Asked a girl what she wanted to be,
She said, baby, can't you see?
I wanna be famous, a star of the screen,
But you can do something in between.

Baby, you can drive my car, yes I'm gonna be a star,
Baby, you can drive my car, and maybe I'll love you.

I told that girl that my prospects were good,
She said, baby, it's understood.
Working for peanuts is all very fine,
But I can show you a better time.

Baby, you can drive my car, yes I'm gonna be a star,
Baby, you can drive my car, and maybe I'll love you.
Beep beep mm beep beep, yeah!

Baby, you can drive my car, yes I'm gonna be a star,
Baby, you can drive my car, and maybe I'll love you.'

I told that girl I could start right away,
And she said, listen, babe, I've got something to say,
I've got no car, and it's breaking my heart,
But I've found a driver, and that's a start.

Baby, you can drive my car, yes I'm gonna be a star,
Baby, you can drive my car, and maybe I'll love you.

Beep beep mm beep beep, yeah!
Beep beep mm beep beep, yeah!
Beep beep mm beep beep, yeah!
Beep beep mm beep beep, yeah!

Norwegian Wood (This Bird Has Flown)

I once had a girl,
Or should I say,
She once had me.
She showed me her room,
Isn't it good
Norwegian wood?

She asked me to stay and she told me to sit anywhere,
So I looked around and I noticed there wasn't a chair.

I sat on a rug,
Biding my time,
Drinking her wine.
We talked until two,
And then she said,
It's time for bed.

She told me she worked in the morning and started to laugh,
I told her I didn't and crawled off to sleep in the bath.

And when I awoke
I was alone,
This bird had flown.
So I lit a fire,
Isn't it good
Norwegian Wood?

You Won't See Me

When I call you up, your line's engaged,
I have had enough, so act your age.
We have lost the time that was so hard to find,
And I will lose my mind
If you won't see me, you won't see me.

I don't know why you should want to hide,
But I can't get through, my hands are tied.
I won't want to stay, I don't have much to say,
But I can turn away,
And you won't see me, you won't see me.

Time after time, you refuse to even listen,
I wouldn't mind if I knew what I was missing.

Though the days are few, they're filled with tears,
And since I lost you, it feels like years,
Yes, it seems so long, girl, since you've been gone,
And I just can't go on,
If you won't see me, you won't see me.

Time after time, you refuse to even listen,
I wouldn't mind if I knew what I was missing.

Though the days are few, they're filled with tears,
And since I lost you, it feels like years,
Yes, it seems so long, girl, since you've been gone,
And I just can't go on,
If you won't see me, you won't see me.

Nowhere Man

He's a real Nowhere Man,
Sitting in his Nowhere Land,
Making all his Nowhere plans for nobody.

Doesn't have a point of view,
Knows not where he's going to,
Isn't he a bit like you and me?

Nowhere Man, please listen,
You don't know what you're missing,
Nowhere Man, the world is at your command.

He's as blind as he can be,
Just sees what he wants to see,
Nowhere Man, can you see me at all?

Nowhere Man, don't worry,
Take your time, don't hurry,
Leave it all till somebody else
Lends you a hand.

Doesn't have a point of view,
Knows not where he's going to,
Isn't he a bit like you and me?

Nowhere Man, please listen,
You don't know what you're missing,
Nowhere Man, the world is at your command.

He's a real Nowhere Man,
Sitting in his Nowhere Land,
Making all his Nowhere plans for nobody.
Making all his Nowhere plans for nobody.
Making all his Nowhere plans for nobody.

Think For Yourself

I've got a word or two
To say about the things that you do.
You're telling all those lies
About the good things that we can have
If we close our eyes.

Do what you want to do,
And go where you're going to,
Think for yourself,
'Cause I won't be there with you.

I left you far behind
The ruins of the life that you have in mind.
And though you still can't see,
I know your mind's made up,
You're gonna cause more misery.

Do what you want to do,
And go where you're going to,
Think for yourself,
'Cause I won't be there with you.

Although your mind's opaque,
Try thinking more,
If just for your own sake.
The future still looks good,
And you've got time to rectify
All the things that you should.

Do what you want to do,
And go where you're going to,
Think for yourself 'cause I won't be there with you.
Do what you want to do,
And go where you're going to,
Think for yourself,
'Cause I won't be there with you.
Think for yourself,
'Cause I won't be there with you.

The Word

Say the word and you'll be free,
Say the word and be like me.
Say the word I'm thinking of,
Have you heard? The word is love.
It's so fine, it's sunshine,
It's the word love.

In the beginning I misunderstood,
But now I've got it, the word is good.

Spread the word and you'll be free,
Spread the word and be like me.
Spread the word I'm thinking of,
Have you heard? The word is love.
It's so fine, it's sunshine,
Its the word love.

Everywhere I go I hear it said,
In the good and the bad books that I have read.

Say the word and you'll be free,
Say the word and be like me.
Say the word I'm thinking of,
Have you heard? The word is love.
It's so fine, it's sunshine,
It's the word love.

Now that I know what I feel must be right,
I mean to show everybody the light,

Give the word a chance to say,
That the word is just the way.
It's the word I'm thinking of,
And the only word is love.
It's so fine, it's sunshine,
It's the word love.

Say the word love,
Say the word love,
Say the word love,
Say the word love.

Michelle

Michell, ma belle,
These are words that go together well,
My Michelle.
Michelle, ma belle,
Sont les mots qui vont très bien ensemble
Très bien ensemble.

I love you, I love you, I love you,
That's all I want to say,
Until I find a way,
I will say the only words I know that you'll understand.

Michelle, ma belle,
Sont les mots qui vont très bien ensemble
Très bien ensemble.

I need to, I need to, I need to,
I need to make you see,
Oh, what you mean to me.
Until I do I'm hoping you will know what I mean:
I love you.

I want you, I want you, I want you,
I think you know by now,
I'll get to you somehow.
Until I do I'm telling you, so you'll understand.

Michelle, ma belle,
Sont les mots qui vont très bien ensemble
Très bien ensemble.
And I will say the only words I know that you'll understand
My Michelle.

What Goes On

What goes on in your heart?
What goes on in your mind?
You are tearing me apart,
When you treat me so unkind.
What goes on in your mind?

The other day I saw you
As I walked along the road.
But when I saw him with you
I could feel my future fold.
It's so easy for a girl like you to lie –
Tell me why.

What goes on in your heart?
What goes on in your mind?
You are tearing me apart,
When you treat me so unkind.
What goes on in your mind?

I met you in the morning,
Waiting for the tides of time.
But now the tide is turning,
I can see that I was blind.
It's so easy for a girl like you to lie –
Tell me why.
What goes on in your heart.

I used to think of no-one else,
But you were jsut the same,
You didn't even think of me
As someone with a name.
Did you mean to break my heart and watch me die?
Tell me why.

What goes on in your heart?
What goes on in your mind?
You are tearing me apart,
When you treat me so unkind.
What goes on in your mind?

Girl

Is there anybody going to listen to my story,
All about the girl who came to stay?
She's the kind of girl you want so much it makes you sorry,
Still, you don't regret a single day.
Ah girl... girl, girl.

When I think of all the times I've tried so hard to leave her,
She will turn to me and start to cry.
And she promises the earth to me and I believe her,
After all this time, I don't know why.
Ah girl... girl, girl.

She's the kind of girl
Who puts you down when friends are there,
You feel a fool.
When you say she's looking good,
She acts as if it's understood,
She's cool, ooh, ooh, ooh,
Girl... girl, girl.

Was she told when she was young that pain would lead to pleasure?
Did she understand it when they said,
That a man must break his back to earn his day of leisure?
Will she still believe it when he's dead?
Ah girl, girl, girl.
Ah girl...

I'm Looking Through You

I'm looking through you, where did you go?
I thought I knew you, what did I know?
You don't look different, but you have changed.
I'm looking through you, you're not the same.

Your lips are moving, I cannot hear,
Your voice is soothing, but the words aren't clear.
You don't sound different, I've learnt the game.
I'm looking through you, you're not the same.

Why, tell me why did you not treat me right?
Love has a nasty habit of disappearing overnight.

You're thinking of me the same old way,
You were above me, but not today.
The only difference is you're down there.
I'm looking through you and you're nowhere.

Why, tell me why did you not treat me right?
Love has a nasty habit of disappearing overnight.

I'm looking through you, where did you go?
I thought I knew you, what did I know?
You don't look different, but you have changed.
I'm looking through you, you're not the same.
Yeah! Well, baby, you've changed.
Ah, I'm looking through you,
Yeah, I'm looking through you...

In My Life

There are places I'll remember
All my life, though some have changed,
Some forever, not for better,
Some have gone and some remain.

All these places had their moments,
With lovers and friends I still can recall,
Some are dead and some are living,
In my life I've loved them all.

But of all these friends and lovers,
There is no one compares with you,
And these memories lose their meaning
When I think of love as something new.

Though I know I'll never lose affection
For people and things that went before,
I know I'll often stop and think about them,
In my life I'll love you more.

Though I know I'll never lose affection
For people and things that went before,
I know I'll often stop and think about them,
In my life I'll love you more.
In my life I'll love you more.

Wait

It's been a long time, now I'm coming back home.
I've been away now, oh, how I've been alone.

Wait till I come back to your side,
We'll forget the tears we cried.

But if your heart breaks, don't wait, turn me away.
And if your heart's strong, hold on, I won't delay.

Wait till I come back to your side,
We'll forget the tears we cried.

I feel as though you ought to know
That I've been good, as good as I can be.
And if you do, I'll trust in you,
And know that you will wait for me.

It's been a long time, now I'm coming back home.
I've been away now, oh, how I've been alone.
Wait till I come back to your side,
We'll forget the tears we cried.

I feel as though you ought to know
That I've been good, as good as I can be.
And if you do, I'll trust in you,
And know that you will wait for me.

But if your heart breaks, don't wait, turn me away.
And if your heart's strong, hold on, I won't delay.

Wait till I come back to your side,
We'll forget the tears we cried.

It's been a long time, now I'm coming back home,
I've been away now, oh, how I've been alone.

If I Needed Someone

If I needed someone to love,
You're the one that I'd be thinking of,
If I needed someone.

If I had some more time to spend,
Then I guess I'd be with you my friend,
If I needed someone.

Had you come some other day,
Then it might not have been like this.
But you see now I'm too much in love.

Carve your number on my wall,
And maybe you will get a call from me,
If I needed someone.

If I had some more time to spend,
Then I guess I'd be with you my friend,
If I needed someone.

Had you come some other day,
Then it might not have been like this.
But you see now I'm too much in love.

Carve your number on my wall,
And maybe you will get a call from me,
If I needed someone.

Run For Your Life

Well, I'd rather see you dead, little girl,
Than to be with another man.
You'd better keep your head, little girl,
Or I won't know where I am.

You'd better run for your life if you can, little girl,
Hide your head in the sand, little girl,
Catch you with another man,
That's the end, little girl.

Well, you know that I'm a wicked guy
And I was born with a jealous mind.
And I can't spend my whole life trying
Just to make you toe the line.

You'd better run for your life if you can, little girl,
Hide your head in the sand, little girl,
Catch you with another man,
That's the end, little girl.

Let this be a sermon,
I mean everything I said,
Baby, I'm determined,
And I'd rather see you dead.

You'd better run for your life if you can, little girl,
Hide your head in the sand, little girl,
Catch you with another man,
That's the end, little girl.

Na, na, na,
Na, na, na,
Na, na, na,
Na, na, na...

Day Tripper

Got a good reason
For taking the easy way out.
Got a good reason
For taking the easy way out, now.

She was a day tripper,
One way ticket, yeah.
It took me so long to find out,
And I found out.

She's a big teaser,
She took me half the way there,
She's a big teaser,
She took me half the way there, now.

She was a day tripper,
One way ticket, yeah.
It took me so long to find out,
And I found out.

Tried to please her,
She only played one night stands.
Tried to please her,
She only played one night stands, now.

She was a day tripper,
Sunday driver, yeah.
It took me so long to find out,
And I found out.

Day tripper, day tripper, yeah.
Day tripper, day tripper, yeah.

We Can Work It Out

Try to see it my way,
Do I have to keep on talking till I can't go on?
While you see it your way,
Run the risk of knowing that our love may soon be gone.

We can work it out,
We can work it out.

Think of what you're saying,
You can get it wrong and still you think that's it's alright.
Think of what I'm saying,
We can work it out and get it straight, or say goodnight.

We can work it out,
We can work it out.

Life is very short, and there's no time
For fussing and fighting, my friend.
I have always thought that it's a crime,
So I will ask you once again.

Try to see it my way,
Only time will tell if I am right or I am wrong.
While you see it your way,
There's a chance that we might fall apart before too long.

We can work it out,
We can work it out.

Life is very short, and there's no time
For fussing and fighting, my friend.
I have always thought that it's a crime,
So I will ask you once again.

Try to see it my way,
Only time will tell if I am right or I am wrong,
While you see it your way,
There's a chance that we might fall apart before too long.

We can work it out,
We can work it out.

Paperback Writer

Paperback writer, paperback writer.

Dear Sir or Madam, will you read my book,
It took me years to write, will you take a look?
It's based on a novel by a man named Lear,
And I need a job,
So I want to be a paperback writer,
Paperback writer.

It's a dirty story of a dirty man,
And his clinging wife doesn't understand.
His son is working for the Daily Mail,
It's a steady job,
But he wants to be a paperback writer,
Paperback writer.

Paperback writer, paperback writer.

It's a thousand pages, give or take a few,
I'll be writing more in a week or two.
I can make it longer if you like the style,
I can change it round,
And I want to be a paperback writer,
Paperback writer.

If you really like it, you can have the rights,
It could make a milllion for you overnight,
If you must return it, you can send it here,
But I need a break,
And I want to be a paperback writer,
Paperback writer.

Paperback writer, paperback writer.

Paperback writer, paperback writer,
Paperback writer, paperback writer...

Rain

If the rain comes, they run and hide their heads.
They might as well be dead,
If the rain comes, if the rain comes.

When the sun shines, they slip into the shade,
And sip their lemonade,
When the sun shines, when the sun shines.

Rain, I don't mind.
Shine, the weather's fine.

I can show you that when it starts to rain,
Everything's the same,
I can show you, I can show you.

Rain, I don't mind.
Shine, the weather's fine.

Can you hear me that when it rains and shines,
It's just a state of mind?
Can you hear me?
Can you hear me?

Taxman

Let me tell you how it will be:
There's one for you, nineteen for me.
'Cause I'm the Taxman,
Yeah, I'm the Taxman.

Should five percent appear too small,
Be thankful I don't take it all.
'Cause I'm the Taxman,
Yeah, I'm the Taxman.

(If you drive a car, car) I'll tax the street,
(If you try to sit, sit) I'll tax your seat,
(If you get too cold, cold) I'll tax the heat,
(If you take a walk, walk) I'll tax your feet...
Taxman!

'Cause I'm the Taxman,
Yeah, I'm the Taxman.

Don't ask me what I want it for
(Ah-ah Mr Wilson!)
If you don't want to pay some more
(Ah-ah Mr Heath!)
'Cause I'm the Taxman,
Yeah, I'm the Taxman.

Now my advice for those who die,
(Taxman!)
Declare the pennies on your eyes.
(Taxman!)
'Cause I'm the Taxman,
Yeah, I'm the Taxman,
And you're working for no-one but me.
(Taxman!)

Eleanor Rigby

Ah, look at all the lonely people!
Ah, look at all the lonely people!

Eleanor Rigby
Picks up the rice in the church where a wedding has been,
Lives in a dream.

Waits at the window,
Wearing a face that she keeps in a jar by the door,
Who is it for?

All the lonely people, where do they all come from?
All the lonely people, where do they all belong?

Father McKenzie,
Writing the words of a sermon that no-one will hear,
No-one comes near.

Look at him working,
Darning his socks in the night
When there's nobody there.
What does he care?

All the lonely people, where do they all come from?
All the lonely people, where do they all belong?

Ah, look at all the lonely people!
Ah, look at all the lonely people!

Eleanor Rigby
Died in the church and was buried along with her name,
Nobody came.

Father McKenzie,
Wiping the dirt from his hands as he walks from her grave,
No-one was saved.

All the lonely people, where do they all come from?
All the lonely people, where do they all belong?

I'm Only Sleeping

When I wake up early in the morning,
Life my head, I'm still yawning.
When I'm in the middle of a dream,
Stay in bed, float upstream (Float upstream).

Please don't wake me, no, don't shake me,
Leave me where I am, I'm only sleeping.

Everybody seems to think I'm lazy.
I don't mind, I think they're crazy,
Running everywhere at such a speed,
Till they find there's no need (There's no need).

Please don't spoil my day, I'm miles away,
And after all, I'm only sleeping.

Keeping an eye on the world going by my window,
Taking my time,
Lying there and staring at the ceiling,
Waiting for a sleepy feeling.

Please don't spoil my day, I'm miles away,
And after all, I'm only sleeping.

Keeping an eye on the world going by my window,
Taking my time,
When I wake up early in the morning,
Lift my head, I'm still yawning.
When I'm in the middle of a dream,
Stay in bed, float upstream (Float upstream).

Please don't wake me, no, don't shake me,
Leave me where I am, I'm only sleeping.

Love You To

Each day just goes so fast,
I turn around, it's past,
You don't get time to hang a sign on me.

Love me while you can,
Before I'm a dead old man.

A lifetime is so short,
A new one can't be bought,
But what you've got means such a lot to me.

Make love all day long,
Make love singing songs.

Make love all day long,
Make love singing songs.

There's people standing round,
Who'll screw you in the ground,
They'll fill you in with all their sins,
You'll see.

I'll make love to you,
If you want me to.

Here There And Everywhere

To lead a better life, I need my love to be here.

Here, making each day of the year,
Changing my life with a wave of her hand,
Nobody can deny that there's something there.

There, running my hands through her hair,
Both of us thinking how good it can be,
Someone is speaking, but she doesn't know he's there.

I want her everywhere,
And if she's beside me I know I need never care,
But to love her is to need her everywhere.

Knowing that love is to share,
Each one believing that love never dies,
Watching their eyes and hoping I'm always there.

I want her everywhere,
And if she's beside me, I know I need never care,
But to love her is to need her everywhere.

Knowing that love is to share,
Each one believing that love never dies,
Watching their eyes and hoping I'm always there.

And we'll be there and everywhere,
Here, there and everywhere.

Yellow Submarine

In the town where I was born,
Lived a man who sailed to sea,
And he told us of his life,
In the land of submarines.

So we sailed on to the sun,
Till we found the sea of green,
And we live beneath the waves,
In our yellow submarine.

We all live in a yellow submarine,
Yellow submarine, yellow submarine.
We all live in a yellow submarine,
Yellow submarine, yellow submarine.

And our friends are all aboard,
Many more of them live next door,
And the band begins to play.

We all live in a yellow submarine,
Yellow submarine, yellow submarine.
We all live in a yellow submarine,
Yellow submarine, yellow submarine.

And we live a life of ease,
Every one of us has all we need,
Sky of blue and sea of green,
In our yellow submarine.

We all live in a yellow submarine,
A yellow submarine, yellow submarine,
We all live in a yellow submarine,
A yellow submarine, yellow submarine.
We all live in a yellow submarine,
Yellow submarine, yellow submarine.

She Said She Said

She said, I know what it's like to be dead,
I know what it is to be sad.
And she's making me feel like I've never been born.

I said, Who put all those things in your head?
Things that make me feel that I'm mad.
And you're making me feel like I've never been born.

She said, You don't understand what I said.
I said, No, no, no, you're wrong,
When I was a boy
Everything was right, everything was right.

I said, Even though you know what you know,
I know that I'm ready to leave,
'Cause you're making me feel like I've never been born.

She said, You don't understand what I said.
I said, No, no, no, you're wrong,
When I was a boy
Everything was right, everything was right.

I said, Even though you know what you know,
I know that I'm ready to leave,
'Cause you're making me feel like I've never been born.

She said, I know what it's like to be dead,
I know what it is to be sad,
I know what it's like to be dead.

Good Day Sunshine

Good day sunshine, good day sunshine,
Good day sunshine.

I need to laugh, and when the sun is out,
I've got something I can laugh about.
I feel good in a special way,
I'm in love, and it's a sunny day.

Good day sunshine, good day sunshine,
Good day sunshine.

We take a walk, the sun is shining down,
Burns my feet as they touch the ground.

Good day sunshine, good day sunshine,
Good day sunshine.

Then we lie beneath a shady tree,
I love her and she's loving me.
She feels good, she knows she's looking fine,
I'm so proud to know that she is mine.

Good day sunshine, good day sunshine,
Good day sunshine.
Good day sunshine, good day sunshine,
Good day sunshine,
Good day sunshine...

And Your Bird Can Sing

You tell me that you've got everything you want,
And your bird can sing,
But you don't get me,
You don't get me.

You say you've seen seven wonders,
And your bird is green,
But you can't see me,
You can't see me.

When your prized possessions
Start to weigh you down,
Look in my direction,
I'll be round, I'll be round.

When your bird is broken,
Will it bring you down?
You may be awoken,
I'll be round, I'll be round.

You tell me that you've heard every sound there is,
And your bird can swing,
But you can't hear me,
You can't hear me.

For No One

Your day breaks, your mind aches,
You find that all her words of kindness linger on
When she no longer needs you.

She wakes up, she makes up,
She takes her time and doesn't feel she has to hurry,
She no longer needs you.

And in her eyes you see nothing,
No sign of love behind the tears cried for no one.
A love that should have lasted years.

You want her, you need her,
And yet, you don't believe her
When she says her love is dead,
You think she needs you.

And in her eyes, you see nothing,
No sign of love behind the tears, cried for no one.
A love that should have lasted years.

You stay home, she goes out,
She says that long ago she knew someone,
But now he's gone,
She doesn't need him.

Your day breaks, your mind aches,
There will be times when all the things she said
Will fill your head,
You won't forget her.

And in her eyes, you see nothing,
No sign of love behind the tears cried for no one.
A love that should have lasted years.

Doctor Robert

Ring my friend, I said you'd call Doctor Robert.
Day or night, he'll be there any time at all,
Doctor Robert.

Doctor Robert,
You're a new and better man,
He helps you to understand,
He does everything he can,
Doctor Robert.

If you're down, he'll pick you up, Doctor Robert.
Take a drink from his special cup, Doctor Robert.

Doctor Robert,
He's a man you must believe,
Helping anyone in need,
No one can succeed like Doctor Robert.

Well, well, well, you're feeling fine,
Well, well, well, he'll make you,
Doctor Robert.

My friend works for the National Health, Doctor Robert.
You'll pay money just to see yourself with Doctor Robert.

Doctor Robert,
You're a new and better man,
He helps you to understand,
He does everything he can,
Doc Robert.

Well, well, well, you're feeling fine,
Well, well, well, he'll make you,
Doctor Robert.

Ring my friend, I said you'd call Doctor Robert.
Ring my friend, I said you'd call Doc Robert.
Doctor Robert!

I Want To Tell You

I want to tell you,
My head is filled with things to say,
When you're here,
All those words they seem to slip away.

When I get near you,
The games begin to drag me down.
It's alright,
I'll make you maybe next time around.

But if I seem to act unkind,
It's only me, it's not my mind,
That is confusing things.

I want to tell you,
I feel hung up and I don't know why.
I don't mind, I could wait forever,
I've got time.

Sometimes I wish I knew you well,
Then I could speak my mind and tell you,
Maybe you'd understand.

I want to tell you,
I feel hung up and I don't know why,
I don't mind, I could wait forever,
I've got time,
I've got time.

Got To Get You Into My Life

I was alone, I took a ride,
I didn't know what I would find there.
Another road where maybe I
Could see another kind of mind there.

Ooh, then I suddenly see you,
Ooh, did I tell you I need you
Every single day of my life?

You didn't run, you didn't lie,
You knew I wanted just to hold you.
And had you gone, you knew in time
We'd meet again, for I had told you.

Ooh, you were meant to be near me,
Ooh, and I want you to hear me
Say we'll be together every day.

Got to get you into my life!

What can I do, what can I be?
When I'm with you, I want to stay there.
If I'm true I'll never leave,
And if I do, I know the way there.

Ooh, then I suddenly see you,
Ooh, did I tell you I need you
Every single day of my life?

Got to get you into my life!

I've got to get you into my life!
I was alone, I took a ride,
I didn't know what I would find there.
Another road where maybe I
Could see another kind of mind there.
Then suddenly I see you,
Did I tell you I need you
Every single day...

Tomorrow Never Knows

Turn off your mind,
Relax and float downstream,
It is not dying, it is not dying.

Lay down all thought,
Surrender to the void,
It is shining, it is shining.

That you may see
The meaning of within,
It is being, it is being.

That love is all
And love is everyone,
It is knowing, it is knowing.

That ignorance and haste
May mourn the dead,
It is believing, it is believing.

But listen to the
Colour of your dreams,
It is not living, it is not living.

Or play the game existence to the end
Of the beginning, of the beginning,
Of the beginning, of the beginning,
Of the beginning, of the beginning,
Of the beginning.

Penny Lane

Penny Lane there is a barber showing photographs
Of every head he's had the pleasure to know.
And all the people that come and go
Stop and say hello.

On the corner is a banker with a motorcar,
The little children laugh at him behind his back.
And the banker never wears a mac
In the pouring rain – very strange.

Penny Lane is in my ears and in my eyes,
There beneath the blue suburban skies
I sit, and meanwhile back

In Penny Lane there is a fireman with an hourglass,
And in his pocket is a portrait of the Queen.
He likes to keep his fire engine clean,
It's a clean machine.

Penny Lane is in my ears and in my eyes,
A four of fish and finger pies
In summer, meanwhile back

Behind the shelter in the middle of the roundabout,
The pretty nurse is selling poppies from a tray.
And though she feels as if she's in a play,
She is anyway.

In Penny Lane the barber shaves another customer,
We see the banker sitting waiting for a trim
And then the fireman rushes in
From the pouring rain – very strange.

Penny Lane is in my ears and in my eyes,
There beneath the blue suburban skies
I sit, and meanwhile back...
Penny Lane is in my ears and in my eyes,
There beneath the blue suburban skies...
Penny Lane.

Strawberry Fields Forever

Let me take you down,
'Cause I'm going to Strawberry Fields.
Nothing is real,
And nothing to get hung about.
Strawberry Fields forever.

Living is easy with eyes closed,
Misunderstanding all you see.
It's getting hard to be someone,
But it all works out;
It doesn't matter much to me.

Let me take you down,
'Cause I'm going to Strawberry Fields.
Nothing is real,
And nothing to get hung about.
Strawberry Fields forever.

No-one I think is in my tree,
I mean, it must be high or low.
That is, you can't, you know, tune in,
But it's all right.
That is, I think it's not too bad.

Let me take you down,
'Cause I'm going to Strawberry Fields.
Nothing is real,
And nothing to get hung about.
Strawberry Fields forever.

Always no, sometimes think it's me,
But you know, I know when it's a dream.
I think I know, I mean a 'Yes',
But it's all wrong.
That is, I think I disagree.

Let me take you down,
'Cause I'm going to Strawberry Fields.
Nothing is real,
And nothing to get hung about.
Strawberry Fields forever.

Sgt. Pepper's Lonely Hearts Club Band

It was twenty years ago today,
Sgt. Pepper taught the band to play.
They've been going in and out of style,
But they're guaranteed to raise a smile.
So may I introduce to you
The act you've know for all these years:
Sgt. Peppers' Lonely Hearts Club Band.

We're Sgt. Pepper's Lonely Hearts Club Band,
We hope you will enjoy the show.
Sgt. Pepper's Lonely Hearts Club Band,
Sit back and let the evening go.
Sgt. Pepper's Lonely, Sgt. Pepper's Lonely,
Sgt. Pepper's Lonely Hearts Club Band.

It's wonderful to be here,
It's certainly a thrill,
You're such a lovely audience,
We'd like to take you home with us,
We'd love to take you home.

I don't really want to stop the show,
But I thought you might like to know,
That the singer's going to sing a song,
And he wants you all to sing along.
So let me introduce to you
The one and only Billy Shears,
And Sgt. Pepper's Lonely Hearts Club Band.

(Billy Shears!)

With A Little Help From My Friends

What would you think if I sang out of tune,
Would you stand up and walk out on me?
Lend me your ears and I'll sing you a song,
And I'll try not to sing out of key.

Oh, I get by with a little help from my friends,
Mmm, I get high with a little help from my friends,
Mmm, gonna try with a little help from my friends.

What do I do when my love is away?
(Does it worry you to be alone?)
How do I feel by the end of the day?
(Are you sad because you're on your own?)

No, I get by with a little help from my friends,
Mmm, I get high with a little help from my friends,
Mmm, gonna try with a little help from my friends.

(Do you need anybody?)
I need somebody to love.
(Could it be anybody?)
I want somebody to love.

(Would you believe in a love at first sight?)
Yes, I'm certain that it happens all the time.
(What do you see when you turn out the light?)
I can't tell you, but I know it's mine.

Oh, I get by with a little help from my friends,
Mmm, get high with a little help from my friends,
Oh, I'm gonna try with a little help from my friends.

(Do you need anybody?)
I just need someone to love.
(Could it be anybody?)
I want somebody to love.

Oh, I get by with a little help form my friends,
Mmm, gonna try with a little help from my friends,
Oh, I get high with a little help from my friends,
Yes, I get by with a little help from my friends,
With a little help from my friends.

Lucy In The Sky With Diamonds

Picture yourself in a boat on a river,
With tangerine trees and marmalade skies.
Somebody calls you, you answer quite slowly,
A girl with kaleidoscope eyes.

Cellophane flowers of yellow and green,
Towering over your head.
Look for the girl with the sun in her eyes,
And she's gone.

Lucy in the sky with diamonds,
Lucy in the sky with diamonds,
Lucy in the sky with diamonds,
Ah-ah.

Follow her down to a bridge by a fountain,
Where rocking horse people eat marshmallow pies.
Everyone smiles as you drift past the flowers,
That grow so incredibly high.

Newspaper taxis appear on the shore,
Waiting to take you away.
Climb in the back with your head in the clouds,
And you're gone.

Lucy in the sky with diamonds,
Lucy in the sky with diamonds,
Lucy in the sky with diamonds,
Ah-ah.

Picture yourself on a train in a station,
With Plasticine porters with looking glass ties.
Suddenly someone is there at the turnstile,
The girl with kaleidoscope eyes.

Lucy in the sky with diamonds,
Lucy in the sky with diamonds,
Lucy in the sky with diamonds,
Ah-ah.

(Repeat and fade.)

Getting Better

It's getting better all the time.

I used to get mad at my school,
The teachers that taught me weren't cool.
You're holding me down, turning me round,
Filling me up with your rules.

I've got to admit, it's getting better,
A little better all the time.
I have to admit, it's getting better,
It's getting better since you've been mine.

Me used to be angry young man,
Me hiding me head in the sand.
You gave me the word,
I finally heard
I'm doing the best that I can.

I've got to admit, it's getting better,
A little better all the time.
I have to admit it's getting better,
It's getting better since you've been mine.
Getting so much better all the time.

It's getting better all the time,
Better, better, better.
It's getting better all the time.
Better, better, better.

I used to be cruel to my woman,
I beat her and kept her apart
From the things that she loved.
Man, I was mean, but I'm changing my scene,
And I'm doing the best that I can.

I admit, it's getting better,
A little better all the time.
Yes, I admit, it's getting better,
It's getting better since you've been mine.
Getting so much better all the time.

It's getting better all the time,

Better, better, better.
It's betting better all the time,
Better, better, better,
Getting so much better all the time.

Fixing A Hole

I'm fixing a hole where the rain gets in,
And stops my mind from wandering
Where it will go.

I'm filling the cracks that ran through the door,
And kept my mind from wandering
Where it will go.

And it really doesn't matter
If I'm wrong, I'm right
Where I belong I'm right
Where I belong.
See the people standing there
Who disagree and never win,
And wonder why they don't get in my door.

I'm painting the room in a colourful way,
And when my mind is wandering,
There I will go.

And it really doesn't matter
If I'm wrong, I'm right
Where I belong I'm right
Where I belong.
Silly people run around,
They worry me
And never ask me why
They don't get past my door.

I'm taking the time for a number of things
That weren't important yesterday,
And I still go.

I'm fixing a hole where the rain gets in
And stops my mind from wandering
Where it will go,
Where it will go.

(Repeat and fade.)

She's Leaving Home

Wednesday morning at five o'clock, as the day begins.
Silently closing her bedroom door,
Leaving the note that she hoped would say more,

She goes downstairs to the kitchen
Clutching her handkerchief.
Quietly turning the backdoor key,
Stepping outside, she is free.

She (We gave her most of our lives)
Is leaving (Sacrificed most of our lives)
Home. (We gave her everything money could buy)
She's leaving home after living alone (Bye, bye)
For so many years.

Father snores as his wife gets into her dressing gown.
Picks up the letter that's lying there,
Standing alone at the top of the stairs,

She breaks down and cries to her husband,
Daddy, our baby's gone.
Why would she treat us so thoughtlessly?
How could she do this to me?

She (We never thought of ourselves)
Is leaving (Never a thought for ourselves)
Home. (We've struggled hard all our lives to get by)
She's leaving home after living alone (Bye, bye)
For so many years.

Friday morning at nine o'clock, she is far away.
Waiting to keep the appointment she made,
Meeting a man from the motor trade.

She (What did we do that was wrong?)
Is having (We didn't know it was wrong)
Fun. (Fun is the one thing that money can't buy)
Something inside that was always denied (Bye, bye)
For so many years.

She's leaving home.
(Bye, bye)

Being For The Benefit Of Mr. Kite!

For the benefit of Mr. Kite,
There will be a show tonight on trampoline.
The Hendersons will all be there,
Late of Pablo Fanques Fair – what a scene!
Over men and horses, hoops and garters,
Lastly throught a hogshead of real fire!
In this way, Mr. K. will challenge the world!

The celebrated Mr. K.
Performs his feat on Saturday at Bishopsgate.
The Hendersons will dance and sing
As Mr. Kite flies through the ring – don't be late!
Messers K. and H. assure the public
Their production will be second to none.
And of course, Henry the Horse dances the waltz!

The band begins at ten to six,
When Mr. K. performs his tricks without a sound.
And Mr. H. will demonstrate
Ten summersets he'll undertake on solid ground.
Having been some days in preparation,
A splendid time is guaranteed for all.
And tonight Mr. Kite is topping the bill.

Within You Without You

We were talking
About the space between us all,
And the people
Who hide themselves behind a wall of illusion,
Never glimpse the truth,
Then it's far too late, when they pass away.

We were talking
About the love we all could share.
When we find it,
To try our best to hold it there.
With our love, with our love
We could save the world – if they only knew.

Try to realise it's all within yourself,
No-one else can make you change.
And to see you're really only very small,
And life flows on within you and without you.

We were talking
About the love that's gone so cold
And the people
Who gain the world and lose their soul.
They don't know,
They can't see,
Are you one of them?

When you've seen beyond yourself,
Then you may find peace of mind is waiting there.
And the time will come when you see we're all one,
And life flows on within you and without you.

When I'm Sixty-Four

When I get older, losing my hair,
Many years from now,
Will you still be sending me a Valentine,
Birthday greetings, bottle of wine?

If I'd been out till quarter to three,
Would you lock the door?
Will you still need me, will you still feed me,
When I'm sixty-four?

You'll be older too.
And if you say the word,
I could stay with you.

I could be handy, mending a fuse
When your lights have gone.
You can knit a sweater by the fireside,
Sunday mornings, go for a ride.

Doing the garden, digging the weeds,
Who could ask for more?
Will you still need me, will you still feed me
When I'm sixty-four?

Every summer we can rent a cottage
In the Isle of Wight, if it's not too dear.
We shall scrimp and save.
Grandchildren on your knee –
Vera, Chuck and Dave.

Send me a postcard, drop me a line,
Stating point of view.
Indicate precisely what you mean to say,
Yours sincerely, wasting away.

Give me your answer, fill in a form,
Mine for evermore.
Will you still need me, will you still feed me,
When I'm sixty-four?

Lovely Rita

Lovely Rita meter maid,
Lovely Rita meter maid.

Lovely Rita meter maid,
Nothing can come between us,
When it gets dark, I tow your heart away.

Standing by a parking meter,
When I caught a glimpse of Rita,
Filling in a ticket in her little white book.

In a cap, she looked much older,
And the bag across her shoulder
Made her look a little like a military man.

Lovely Rita meter maid,
May I inquire discreetly,
When are you free
To take some tea with me?
(Rita!)

Took her out and tried to win her,
Had a laugh, and over dinner
Told her I would really like to see her again.

Got the bill and Rita paid it,
Took her home, I nearly made it,
Sitting on a sofa with a sister or two.

Oh, lovely Rita meter maid,
Where would I be without you?
Give us a wink and make me think of you

Lovely Rita meter maid,
Lovely Rita meter maid.

(Repeat and fade.)

Good Morning, Good Morning

Good morning, good morning,
Good morning, good morning,
Good morning-ah!

Nothing to do to save his life, call his wife in.
Nothing to say but what a day, how's your boy been?
Nothing to do, it's up to you.
I've got nothing to say, but it's O.K.
(Good morning, good morning,
Good morning-ah!)

Going to work, don't want to go, feeling low down.
Heading for home you start to roam, then you're in town.

Everybody knows there's nothing doing,
Everything is closed, it's like a ruin,
Everyone you see is half-asleep,
And you're on your own, you're in the street.

After a while you start to smile, now you feel cool.
Then you decide to take a walk by the old shcool.
Nothing has changed, it's still the same,
I've got nothing to say, but it's O.K.
(Good morning, good morning,
Good morning-ah!)

People running round, it's five o'clock,
Everywhere in town is getting dark,
Everyone you see is full of life,
It's time for tea and 'Meet the Wife'.

Somebody needs to know the time, glad that I'm here.
Watching the skirts, you start to flirt, now you're in gear.
Go to a show, you hope she goes,
I've got nothing to say, but it's O.K.
(Good morning, good morning, good!
Good morning, good morning, good!)

(Repeat and fade.)

Sgt. Pepper's Lonely Hearts Club Band (Reprise)

We're Sgt. Pepper's Lonely Hearts Club Band,
We hope you have enjoyed the show.
Sgt. Pepper's Lonely Hearts Club Band,
We're sorry, but it's time to go.
Sgt. Pepper's Lonely, Sgt. Pepper's Lonely,
Sgt. Pepper's Lonely, Sgt. Pepper's Lonely.

Sgt. Pepper's Lonely Hearts Club Band,
We'd like to thank you once again.
Sgt. Pepper's one and only Lonely Hearts Club Band,
It's getting very near the end.
Sgt. Pepper's Lonely, Sgt. Pepper's Lonely,
Sgt. Pepper's Lonely Hearts Club Band.

A Day In The Life

I read the news today, oh boy,
About a lucky man who made the grade.
And though the news was rather sad,
Well, I just had to laugh.
I saw the photograph.

He blew his mind out in a car;
He didn't notice that the lights had changed.
A crowd of people stood and stared.
They'd seen his face before,
Nobody was really sure
If he was from the House of Lords.

I saw a film today, oh boy,
The English Army had just won the war.
A crowd of people turned away,
But I just had to look,
Having read the book.
I'd love to turn you on.

Woke up, fell out of bed,
Dragged a comb across my head.
Found my way downstairs and drank a cup,
And looking up, I noticed I was late.

Found my coat and grabbed my hat,
Made the bus in seconds flat.
Found my way upstairs and had a smoke.
And somebody spoke and I went into a dream.

(Ah...)

I read the news today, oh boy,
Four thousand holes in Blackburn, Lancashire.
And though the holes were rather small,
They had to count them all.
Now they know how many holes
It takes to fill the Albert Hall.
I'd love to turn you on.

All You Need Is Love

Love, love, love,
Love, love, love,
Love, love, love.

There's nothing you can do that can't be done,
Nothing you can sing that can't be sung,
Nothing you can say, but you can learn how to play the game –
It's easy.

Nothing you can make that can't be made,
No-one you can save that can't be saved,
Nothing you can do, but you can learn how to be you in time –
It's easy.

All you need is love,
All you need is love,
All you need is love, love,
Love is all you need.

Love, love, love,
Love, love, love,
Love, love love.

All you need is love,
All you need is love,
All you need is love, love,
Love is all you need.

There's nothing you can know that isn't known,
Nothing you can see that isn't shown,
There's nowhere you can be that isn't where you're meant to be –
It's easy.

All you need is love,
All you need is love,
All you need is love, love,
Love is all you need.

All you need is love,
All you need is love,
All you need is love, love,
Love is all you need.

Love is all you need,
Love is all you need.

(Repeat and fade.)

Baby You're A Rich Man

How does it feel to be one of the beautiful people?
Now that you know who you are,
What do you want to be?
And have you travelled very far?
Far as the eye can see.

How does it feel to be one of the beautiful people?
How often have you been there?
Often enough to know.
What did you see when you were there?
Nothing that doesn't show.

Baby you're a rich man,
Baby you're a rich man,
Baby you're a rich man too.
You keep all your money in a big brown bag
Inside a zoo.
What a thing to do.
Baby you're a rich man,
Baby you're a rich man,
Baby you're a rich man too.

How does it feel to be one of the beautiful people?
Tuned to a natural E,
Happy to be that way.
Now that you've found another key,
What are you going to play?

Baby you're a rich man,
Baby you're a rich man,
Baby you're a rich man too.
You keep all your money in a big brown bag
Inside a zoo.
What a thing to do.

Baby, baby you're a rich man,
Baby you're a rich man,
Baby you're a rich man too...

Hello, Goodbye

You say yes, I say no,
You say stop, but I say go, go, go.
Oh no.
You say goodbye and I say hello.

Hello, hello,
I don't know why you say goodbye, I say hello,
Hello, hello,
I don't know why you say goodbye, I say hello.

I say high, you say low,
You say why and I say I don't know.
Oh no.
You say goodbye and I say hello,
(Hello, goodbye, hello, goodbye)

Hello, hello, (Hello, goodbye)
I don't know why you say goodbye, I say hello,
(Hello, goodbye, hello, goodbye)
Hello, hello,
(Hello, goodbye)
I don't know why you say goodbye I say hello. (Hello, goodbye)

Why, why, why, why, why, why,
Do you say goodbye, goodbye?
Oh no.
You say goodbye and I say hello,

Hello, hello,
I don't know why you say goodbye, I say hello,
Hello, hello,
I don't know why you say goodbye, I say hello.

You say yes, I say no (I say yes, but I may mean no)
You say stop, but I say go, go, go, (I can stay till it's time to go)
Oh, oh no.
You say goodbye and I say hello,

Hello, hello,
I don't know why you say goodbye, I say hello,
Hello, hello,
I don't know why you say goodbye, I say hello,

Hello, hello,
I don't know why you say goodbye
I say hello,
Hello.

Hela, heba, helloa,
Hela, heba, helloa,
Hela, heba, helloa,
Hela, heba, helloa...

I Am The Walrus

I am he
As you are he
As you are me
And we are all together.
See how they run,
Like pigs from a gun,
See how they fly.
I'm crying.

Sitting on a cornflake,
Waiting for the van to come.
Corporation T shirt
Stupid bloody Tuesday man, you been a naughty boy,
You let your face grow long.

I am the eggman, they are the eggmen,
I am the walrus,
GOO GOO G'JOOB.

Mr. City policmen,
Sitting pretty little policemen in a row.
See how they fly,
Like Lucy in the sky,
See how they run.
I'm crying.

I'm crying,
I'm crying, I'm crying.

Yellow matter custard,
Dripping from a dead dog's eye.
Crabalocker fishwife, pornographic priestess,
Boy, you been a naughty girl,
You let your knickers down.
I am the eggman, they are the eggmen,
I am the walrus,
GOO GOO G'JOOB.

Sitting in an English garden, waiting for the sun.
If the sun don't come, you get a tan
From standing in the English rain.
I am the eggman, they are the eggmen,

I am the walrus,
GOO GOO G'JOOB,
GOO GOO GOO G'JOOB.

Expert texpert choking smokers,
Don't you think the joker laughs at you?
(Ha ha ha! Hee hee hee! Ha ha ha!)
See how they smile,
Like pigs in the sty,
See how they snied.
I'm crying.

Semolina pilchard,
Climbing up the Eiffel Tower.
Elementary penguin singing Hare Krishna,
Man, you should have seen them
Kicking Edgar Allen Poe.

I am the eggman,
They are the eggmen,
I am the walrus,
GOO GOO G'JOOB,
GOO GOO GOO G'JOOB,
GOO GOO G'JOOB,
GOO GOO GOO G'JOOB
GOO GOO,
JOOB JOOB JOOB...

Magical Mystery Tour

(Roll up, roll up for the Magical Mystery Tour –
Step right this way!)

Roll up – roll up for the Mystery Tour.
Roll up – roll up for the Mystery Tour.
Roll up (And that's an invitation)
Roll up for the Mystery Tour
Roll up (To make a reservation)
Roll up for the Mystery Tour.

The Magical Mystery Tour
Is waiting to take you away,
Waiting to take you away.

Roll up – roll up for the Mystery Tour.
Roll up – roll up for the Mystery Tour.
Roll up (We've got everything you need)
Roll up for the Mystery Tour.
Roll up (Satisfaction guaranteed)
Roll up for the Mystery Tour.

The Magical Mystery Tour
Is hoping to take you away.
Hoping to take you away.

(Mystery trip)

Now... the Magical Mystery Tour,
Roll up – roll up for the Mystery Tour,
Roll up (And that's an invitation)
Roll up for the Mystery Tour.
Roll up (To make a reservation)
Roll up for the Mystery Tour.

The Magical Mystery Tour
Is coming to take you away,
Coming to take you away.

The Magical Mystery Tour
Is dying to take you away,
Dying to take you away,
Take you today.

The Fool On The Hill

Day after day, alone on a hill,
The man with the foolish grin is keeping perfectly still.
But nobody wants to know him,
They can see that he's just a fool.
And he never gives an answer,
But the fool on the hill
Sees the sun going down,
And the eyes in his head
See the world spinning round.

Well on the way, head in a cloud,
The man of a thousand voices talking perfectly loud.
But nobody ever hears him,
Or the sound he appears to make.
And he never seems to notice,
But the fool on the hill
Sees the sun going down,
And the eyes in his head
See the world spinning round.

And nobody seems to like him,
They can tell what he wants to do.
And he never shows his feelings,
But the fool on the hill
Sees the sun going down,
And the eyes in his head
See the world spinning round.

(Oh...
Round and round and round and
round and round)

And he never listens to them,
He knows that they're the fool.
They don't like him,
The fool on the hill
Sees the sun going down,
And the eyes in his head
See the world spinning round.

(Oh...
Round and round and round and

round and...
Oh...
Round and round and round and
round)

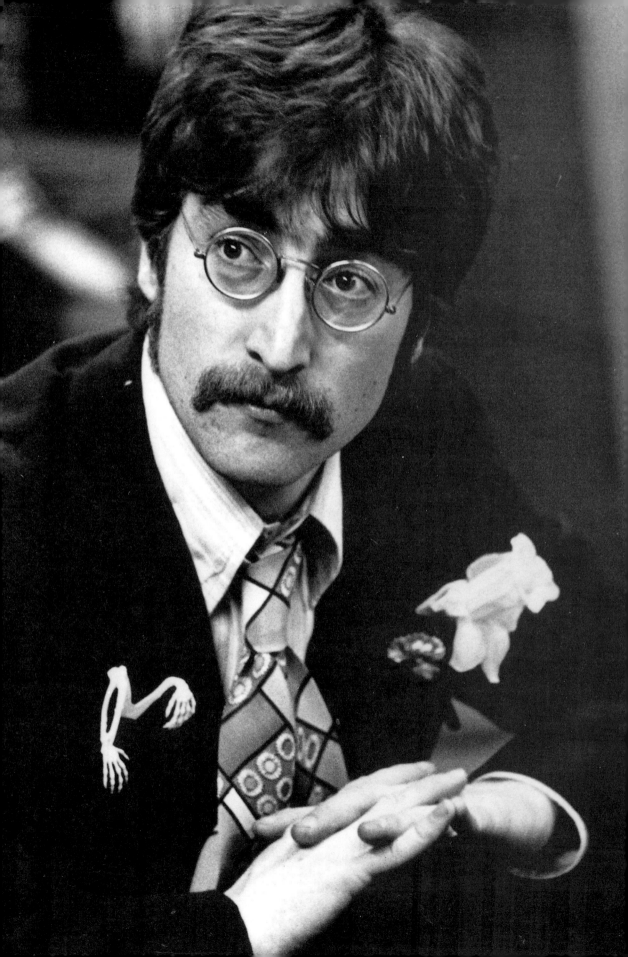

Blue Jay Way

There's a fog upon L.A.
And my friends have lost their way.
We'll be over soon, they said,
Now they've lost themselves instead.

Please don't be long,
Please don't you be very long,
Please don't be long,
Or I may be asleep.

Well, it only goes to show,
And I told them where to go:
Ask a policeman on the street,
There's so many there to meet.

Please don't be long,
Please don't you be very long,
Please don't be long,
Or I may be asleep.

Now it's past my bed, I know,
And I'd really like to go.
Soon will be the break of day,
Sitting here in Blue Jay Way.

Please don't be long,
Please don't you be very long,
Please don't be long,
Or I may be asleep.
Please don't be long,
Please don't you be very long,
Please don't be long.

Please don't be long,
Please don't you be very long,
Please don't be long.

Please don't be long,
Please don't you be very long,
Please don't be long.

Don't be long, don't be long,
Don't be long,
Don't be long...

Your Mother Should Know

Let's all get up and dance to a song
That was a hit before your mother was born.
Though she was born a long, long time ago,
Your mother should know,
Your mother should know.

Sing it again.
Let's all get up and dance to a song
That was a hit before your mother was born.
Though she was born a long, long time ago,
Your mother should know,
Your mother should know.

Lift up your hearts and sing me a song
That was a hit before your mother was born.
Though she was born a long, long time ago,
Your mother should know,
Your mother should know.
Your mother should know,
Your mother should know.

Sing it again...
Though she was born a long, long time ago,
Your mother should know, your mother should know.
Your mother should know, your mother should know.
Your mother should know, your mother should know.

Lady Madonna

Lady Madonna, children at your feet,
Wonder how you manage to make ends meet.
Who finds the money when you pay the rent?
Did you think that money was heaven sent?

Friday night arrives without a suitcase,
Sunday morning, creeping like a nun.
Monday's child has learned to tie his bootlace.
See how they run.

Lady Madonna, baby at your breast,
Wonders how you manage to feed the rest.

See how they run.

Lady Madonna, lying on the bed,
Listen to the music playing in your head.

Tuesday afternoon is never-ending,
Wednesday morning, papers didn't come.
Thursday night, your stockings needed mending:
See how they run.

Lady Madonna, children at your feet,
Wonder how you manage to make ends meet.

The Inner Light

Without going out of my door,
I can know all things on earth.
Without looking out of my window,
I can know the ways of heaven.

The farther one travels,
The less one knows.
The less one really knows.

Without going out of your door,
You can know all things on earth.
Without looking out of your window,
You can know the ways of heaven.

The farther one travels,
The less one knows.
The less one really knows.

Arrive without travelling.
See all without looking,
Do all without doing.

Hey Jude

Hey Jude, don't make it bad,
Take a sad song and make it better.
Remember to let her into your heart,
Then you can start to make it better.

Hey Jude, don't be afraid,
You were made to go out and get her.
The minute you let her under your skin,
Then you begin to make it better.

And any time you feel the pain,
Hey Jude, refrain,
Don't carry the world upon your shoulder.
For well you know that it's a fool who plays it cool
By making his world a little colder.
Na na-na na na,
Na-na na na.

Hey Jude, don't let me down,
You have found her, now go and get her.
Remember
To let her into your heart,
Then you can start to make it better.

So let it out and let it in,
Hey Jude, begin,
You're waiting for someone to perform with.
And don't you know that it's just you,
Hey Jude, you'll do,
The movement you need is on your shoulder.
Na na-na na na,
Na-na na na, yeah.

Hey Jude, don't make it bad,
Take a sad song and make it better.
Remember to let her under your skin,
Then you begin to make it better,
Better, better, better,
Better, better, ah!

Na na na na-na-na na,
Na-na-na na,
Hey Jude...

Revolution

You say you want a revolution,
Well, you know,
We all want to change the world.
You tell me that it's evolution,
Well, you know,
We all want to change the world.

But when you talk about destruction,
Don't you know that you can count me out.

Don't you know it's going to be alright,
Alright, alright.

You say you got a real solution,
Well, you know,
We'd all love to see the plan.
You ask me for a contribution,
Well, you know,
We're all doing what we can.

But if you want money for people with minds that hate,
All I can tell you is, brother, you'll have to wait.

Don't you know it's going to be alright,
Alright, alright.

You say you'll change the constitution,
Well, you know,
We all want to change your head.
You tell me it's the institution,
Well, you know,
You'd better free your mind instead.

But if you go carrying pictures of Chairman Mao,
You ain't gonna make it with anyone anyhow.

Don't you know it's going to be alright,
Alright, alright.

Alright, alright,
Alright, alright,
Alright, alright,
Alright, alright!

Back In The U.S.S.R.

Flew in from Miami Beach BOAC,
Didn't get to bed last night.
On the way the paper bag was on my knee,
Man, I had a dreadful flight.

I'm back in the U.S.S.R.
You don't know how lucky you are, boy,
Back in the U.S.S.R.

Been away so long I hardly knew the place,
Gee, it's good to be back home.
Leave it till tomorrow to unpack my case,
Honey, disconnect the phone.

I'm back in the U.S.S.R.
You don't know how lucky you are, boy.
Back in the U.S., back in the U.S.,
Back in the U.S.S.R.

Well, the Ukraine girls really knock me out,
They leave the West behind,
And Moscow girls make me sing and shout,
That Georgia's always on my my my
My my my my my my mind.
(Oh come on!)

I'm back in the U.S.S.R.,
You don't know how lucky you are, boys,
Back in the U.S.S.R.

Well, the Ukraine girls really knock me out,
They leave the West behind,
And Moscow girls make me sing and shout,
That Georgia's always on my my my
My my my my my my mind.

Oh, show me round your snow-peaked mountains
Way down south,
Take me to your daddy's farm,
Let me hear your balalaikas ringing out,
Come and keep your comrade warm.

I'm back in the U.S.S.R.
You don't know how lucky you are, boy,
Back in the U.S.S.R.

(Oh, let me tell you honey...)

Dear Prudence

Dear Prudence, won't you come out to play?
Dear Prudence, greet the brand new day.

The sun is up, the sky is blue,
It's beautiful and so are you,
Dear Prudence, won't you come out to play?

Dear Prudence, open up your eyes.
Dear Prudence, see the sunny skies.

The wind is low, the birds will sing,
That you are part of everything,
Dear Prudence, won't you open up your eyes?

Look around round (round, round round,
Round round round round round),
Look around round round (round round,
Round round round round round),
Look around.

Dear Prudence, let me see you smile.
Dear Prudence, like a little child.
The clouds will be a daisy chain,
So let me see you smile again,
Dear Prudence, won't you let me see you smile?

Dear Prudence, won't you come out to play?
Dear Prudence, greet the brand new day.

The sun is up, the sky is blue,
It's beautiful and so are you,
Dear Prudence, won't you come out to play?

Glass Onion

I told you 'bout Strawberry Fields,
You know, the place where nothing is real.
Well, here's another place you can go
Where everything flows.

Looking through the bent-backed tulips
To see how the other half live,
Looking through a glass onion.

I told you 'bout the walrus and me, man,
You know that we're as close as can be, man,
Well, here's another clue for you all –
The walrus was Paul.

Standing on the cast iron shore, yeah,
Lady Madonna trying to make ends meet, yeah,
Looking through a glass onion.

Oh yeah, oh yeah, oh yeah!
Looking through a glass onion.

I told you 'bout the fool on the hill,
I tell you man, he's living there still,
Well here's another place you can be –
Listen to me.

Fixing a hole in the ocean,
Trying to make a dovetail joint, yeah,
Looking through a glass onion.

Ob-La-Di, Ob-La-Da

Desmond has a barrow in the market place,
Molly is the singer in a band.
Desmond says to Molly,
Girl, I like your face,
And Molly says this as she takes him by the hand:

Ob-La-Di, Ob-La-Da, life goes on, Bra,
La-la how their life goes on.
Ob-La-Di, Ob-La-Da, life goes on, Bra,
La-la how their life goes on.

Desmond takes a trolley to the jeweller's store,
Buys a twenty carat golden ring.
Takes it back to Molly waiting at the door,
And as he gives it to her, she begins to sing:

Ob-La-Di, Ob-La-Da, life goes on, Bra,
La-la how their life goes on.
Ob-La-Di, Ob-La-Da, life goes on, Bra,
La-la how their life goes on.

In a couple of years, they have built
A home sweet home.
With a couple of kids running in the yard
Of Desmond and Molly Jones.

Happy ever after in the market place,
Desmond lets the children lend a hand.
Molly stays at home and does her pretty face,
And in the evening she still sings it with the band.

Yes, Ob-La-Di, Ob-La-Da, life goes on, Bra,
La-la how their life goes on.
Ob-La-Di, Ob-La-Da, life goes on, Bra,
La-la how their life goes on.

In a couple of years, they have built
A home sweet home.
With a couple of kids running in the yard
Of Desmond and Molly Jones.

Happy ever after in the market place,

Molly lets the children lend a hand.
Desmond stays at home and does his pretty face,
And in the evening she's a singer with the band.

Yeah, Ob-La-Di, Ob-La-Da, life goes on, Bra,
La-la how their life goes on.
Yeah, Ob-La-Di, Ob-La-Da, life goes on, Bra,
La-la how their life goes on.

And if you want some fun, take Ob-La-Di-Bla-Da.

Wild Honey Pie

Honey Pie,
Honey Pie,
Honey Pie.

Honey Pie,
Honey Pie,
Honey Pie.

Honey Pie,
Honey Pie,
Honey Pie,
Honey Pie,
I love you, Honey Pie.

The Continuing Story Of Bungalow Bill

Hey, Bungalow Bill,
What did you kill,
Bungalow Bill?
Hey, Bungalow Bill,
What did you kill,
Bungalow Bill?

He went out tiger hunting, with his elephant and gun.
In case of accidents, he always took his mom.
He's the all-American, bullet-headed,
Saxon mother's son.

(All the children sing!)

Hey, Bungalow Bill,
What did you kill,
Bungalow Bill?
Hey, Bungalow Bill,
What did you kill,
Bungalow Bill?

Deep in the jungle, where the mighty tiger lies,
Bill and his elephants were taken by surprise.
So Captain Marvel zapped him right between the eyes.

(All the children sing!)

Hey, Bungalow Bill,
What did you kill,
Bungalow Bill?
Hey, Bungalow Bill,
What did you kill,
Bungalow Bill?

The children asked him if to kill was not a sin:
Not when he looks so fierce, his mommy butted in.
If looks could kill, it would have been
Us instead of him.

(All the children sing!)

Hey, Bungalow Bill,

What did you kill,
Bungalow Bill?
Hey, Bungalow Bill,
What did you kill,
Bungalow Bill...

While My Guitar Gently Weeps

I look at you all, see the love there that's sleeping,
While my guitar gently weeps.
I look at the floor, and I see it needs sweeping,
Still my guitar gently weeps.

I don't know why nobody told you
How to unfold your love.
I don't know how someone controlled you –
They bought and sold you.

I look at the world and I notice it's turning,
While my guitar gently weeps.
With every mistake, we must surely be learning,
Still my guitar gently weeps.

I don't know how you were diverted,
You were perverted too.
I don't know how you were inverted –
No one alerted you.

I look at you all, see the love there that's sleeping,
While my guitar gently weeps.
I look at you all.
Still my guitar gently weeps.

Happiness Is A Warm Gun

She's not a girl who misses much.
Do-do-do-do-do-do do, oh yeah.

She's well acquainted with the touch
Of the velvet hand,
Like a lizard on a window pane.
The man in the crowd,
With the multicoloured mirrors on his hobnail boots.
Lying with his hands,
While his hands are busy working overtime.
A soap impression of his wife, which he ate,
And donated to the National Trust.

I need a fix, 'cause I'm going down,
Down to the bits that I left uptown,
I need a fix, 'cause I'm going down.

Mother Superior, jump the gun,
Mother Superior, jump the gun,
Mother Superior, jump the gun,
Mother Superior, jump the gun,
Mother Superior, jump the gun,
Mother Superior, jump the gun.

Happiness is a warm gun, (Bang, bang, shoot, shoot)
Happiness is a warm gun, momma. (Bang, bang, shoot, shoot)
When I hold you in my arms, (Ooh, oh yeah)
And I feel my finger on your trigger, (Ooh, oh yeah)
I know nobody can do me no harm, (Ooh, oh yeah)

Because –
Happiness is a warm gun, momma, (Bang, bang, shoot, shoot)
Happiness is a warm gun, yes it is, (Bang bang, shoot, shoot)
Happiness is a warm, yes it is...

Gun! (Happiness... Bang, bang, shoot, shoot)
Well, don't you know that happiness
Is a warm gun, yeah.
(Happiness... is a warm gun, yeah)

Martha My Dear

Martha my dear,
Though I spend my days in conversation,
Please remember me.

Martha my love,
Don't forget me,
Martha my dear.

Hold your head up, you silly girl,
Look what you've done.
When you find yourself in the thick of it,
Help yourself to a bit of what is all around you,
Silly girl.

Take a good look around you,
Take a good look, you're bound to see
That you and me
Were meant to be for each other,
Silly girl.

Hold your hand out, you silly girl,
See what you've done.
When you find yourself in the thick of it,
Help yourself to a bit of what is all around you,
Silly girl.

Martha my dear,
You have always been my inspiration,
Please be good to me.

Martha my love,
Don't forget me,
Martha my dear.

I'm So Tired

I'm so tired, I haven't slept a wink,
I'm so tired, my mind is on the blink.
I wonder should I get up
And fix myself a drink?
No, no, no.

I'm so tired, I don't know what to do,
I'm so tired – my mind is set on you.
I wonder should I call you,
But I know what you would do.

You'd say I'm putting you on,
But it's no joke, it's doing me harm,
You know I can't sleep, I can't stop my brain,
You know it's three weeks, I'm going insane,
You know I'd give you everything I've got
For a little peace of mind.

I'm so tired, I'm feeling so upset,
Although I'm so tired, I'll have another cigarette,
And curse Sir Walter Raleigh,
He was such a stupid get.

You'd say I'm putting you on,
But it's no joke, it's doing me harm,
You know I can't sleep, I can't stop my brain,
You know it's three weeks, I'm going insane,
You know I'd give you everything I've got
For a little peace of mind.
I'd give you everything I've got
For a little peace of mind.
I'd give you everything I've got
For a little peace of mind.

Blackbird

Blackbird singing in the dead of night,
Take these broken wings and learn to fly.
All your life,
You were only waiting for this moment to arise.

Blackbird singing in the dead of night,
Take these sunken eyes and learn to see.
All your life,
You were only waiting for this moment to be free.

Blackbird, fly,
Blackbird, fly
Into the light of a dark black night.

Blackbird, fly,
Blackbird, fly
Into the light of a dark black night.

Blackbird singing in the dead of night,
Take these broken wings and learn to fly.
All your life,
You were only waiting for this moment to arise.
You were only waiting for this moment to arise.
You were only waiting for this moment to arise.

Piggies

Have you seen the little piggies crawling in the dirt?
And for all the little piggies, life is getting worse,
Always having dirt to play around in.

Have you seen the bigger piggies in their starched white shirts?
You will find the bigger piggies stirring up the dirt
Always have clean shirts to play around in.

In their styes with all their backing,
They don't care what goes on around.
In their eyes there's something lacking –
What they need's a damn good whacking!

Everywhere there's lots of piggies, living piggy lives,
You can see them out for dinner with their piggy wives,
Clutching forks and knives to eat their bacon.

Rocky Raccoon

Now somewhere in the black mountain hills of Dakota
There lived a young boy named Rocky Raccoon.
And one day his woman ran off with another guy,
Hit young Rocky in the eye,
Rocky didn't like that,
He said, I'm gonna get that boy.
So one day he walked into town,
Booked himself a room in the local saloon.

Rocky Raccoon checked into his room,
Only to find Gideon's Bible.
Rocky had come, equipped with a gun,
To shoot off the legs of his rival.
His rival, it seems, had broken his dreams,
By stealing the girl of his fancy.
Her name was Magill, and she called herself Lil,
But everyone knew her as Nancy.

Now she and her man,
Who called himself Dan,
Were in the next room at the hoe down.
Rocky burst in,
And grinning a grin,
He said, Danny boy, this is a showdown.
But Daniel was hot –
He drew first and shot,
And Rocky collapsed in the corner.

Now, the doctor came in, stinking of gin,
And proceeded to lie on the table.
He said, Rocky, you met your match,
And Rocky said, Doc, it's only a scratch,
And I'll be better, I'll be better, Doc,
As soon as I am able.

Now Rocky Raccoon
He fell back in his room,
Only to find Gideon's Bible.
Gideon checked out
And he left in no doubt
To help with good Rocky's revival.

Don't Pass Me By

I listen for your footsteps coming up the drive,
Listen for your footsteps, but they don't arrive.
Waiting for your knock, dear, on my old front door,
I don't hear it,
Does it mean you don't love me anymore?

I hear the clock a-ticking on the mantel shelf,
See the hands a-moving, but I'm by myself.
I wonder where you are tonight and why I'm by myself,
I don't see you,
Does it mean you don't love me anymore?

Don't pass me by, don't make me cry,
Don't make me blue.
'Cause you know, darling, I love only you.
You'll never know it hurt me so,
I hate to see you go,
Don't pass me by, don't make me cry.

I'm sorry that I doubted you, I was so unfair,
You were in a car crash, and you lost your hair.
You said that you would be late, about an hour or two,
I say that's alright, I'm waiting here, just waiting to hear from you.

Don't pass me by, don't make me cry,
Don't make me blue.
'Cause you know, darling, I love only you.
You'll never know it hurt me so,
How I hate to see you go,
Don't pass me by, don't make me cry.

Don't pass me by, don't make me cry,
Don't make me blue.
'Cause you know, darling, I love only you.
You'll never know it hurt me so,
How I hate to see you go,
Don't pass me by, don't make me cry.

Why Don't We Do It In The Road

Why don't we do it in the road?
Why don't we do it in the road?
Why don't we do it in the road?
Why don't we do it in the road?
No one will be watching us,
Why don't we do it in the road?

Why don't we do it in the road?
Why don't we do it in the road?
Why don't we do it in the road?
Why don't we do it in the road?
No one will be watching us,
Why don't we do it in the road?

Why don't we do it in the road?
Why don't we do it in the road?
Why don't we do it, do it in the road?
Why don't we do it in the road?
No one will be watching us,
Why don't we do it in the road?

I Will

Who knows how long I've loved you?
You know I love you still,
Will I wait a lonely lifetime?
If you want me to, I will.

For if I ever saw you,
I didn't catch your name.
But it never really mattered –
I will always feel the same.

Love you forever and forever,
Love you with all my heart,
Love you whenever we're together,
Love you when we're apart.

And when at last I find you,
Your song will fill the air.
Sing it loud so I can hear you,
Make it easy to be near you,
For the things you do endear you to me
Oh, you know I will,
I will.

Julia

Half of what I say is meaningless,
But I say it just to reach you, Julia.

Julia, Julia, ocean child, calls me,
So I sing a song of love, Julia.
Julia, seashell eyes, windy smile, calls me,
So I sing a song of love, Julia.

Her hair of floating sky is shimmering,
Glimmering,
In the sun.

Julia, Julia, morning moon, touch me,
So I sing a song of love, Julia.

When I cannot sing my heart,
I can only speak my mind, Julia.

Julia, sleeping sand, silent cloud, touch me,
So I sing a song of love, Julia.

Mm-mm-mm...
... calls me,
So I sing a song of love for Julia,
Julia,
Julia.

Birthday

You say it's your birthday,
It's my birthday too, yeah.
You say it's your birthday,
We're gonna have a good time.
I'm glad it's your birthday,
Happy birthday to you.

Yes, we're going to a party, party,
Yes, we're going to a party, party,
Yes, we're going to a party, party.

I would like you to dance,
(Birthday) Take a cha-cha-cha-chance,
(Birthday) I would like you to dance,
(Birthday) Dance!

I would like you to dance,
(Birthday) Take a cha-cha-cha-chance,
(Birthday) I would like you to dance,
(Birthday) Dance!

You say it's your birthday,
It's my birthday too, yeah.
You say it's your birthday,
We're gonna have a good time.
I'm glad it's your birthday,
Happy birthday to you.

Yer Blues

Yes, I'm lonely, wanna die,
Yes, I'm lonely, wanna die,
If I ain't dead already,
Whoo – girl, you know the reason why.

In the morning, wanna die,
In the evening, wanna die,
If I ain't dead already,
Whoo – girl, you know the reason why.

My mother was of the sky,
My father was of the earth,
But I am of the universe,
And you know what it's worth.

I'm lonely, wanna die,
If I ain't dead already,
Whoo – girl, you know the reason why.

The eagle picks my eye,
The worm, he licks my bone,
Feel so suicidal,
Just like Dylan's Mr. Jones.

Lonely, wanna die,
If I ain't dead already,
Whoo – girl, you know the reason why.

Black cloud crossed my mind,
Blue mist round my soul,
Feel so suicidal,
Even hate my rock and roll.

Wanna die,
Yeah, wanna die,
If I ain't dead already,
Whoo – girl, you know the reason why.

(Yes, I'm lonely, wanna die,
Yes, I'm lonely, wanna die,
If I ain't dead already,
Girl, you know the reason why.)

Mother Nature's Son

Born a poor young country boy,
Mother Nature's son.
All day long I'm sitting singing songs for everyone.

Sit beside a mountain stream,
See her waters rise,
Listen to the pretty sound of music as she flies.

Find me in my field of grass,
Mother Nature's son,
Swaying daisies sing a lazy song beneath the sun.

Mother Nature's son.

Everybody's Got Something To Hide
Except For Me And My Monkey

Come on, come on.
Come on, come on,
Come on is such a joy,
Come on is such a joy,
Come on is take it easy,
Come on is take it easy.

Take it easy.
Take it easy.
Everybody's got something to hide,
Except for me and my monkey.

The deeper you go, the higher you fly,
The higher you fly, the deeper you go,
So come on, come on.
Come on is such a joy,
Come on is such a joy,
Come on is make it easy,
Come on is make it easy.

Take it easy.
Take it easy.
Everybody's got something to hide,
Except for me and my monkey.

Your inside is out when your outside is in,
Your outside is in when your inside is out,
So come on, come on.
Come on is such a joy,
Come on is such a joy,
Come on is make it easy,
Come on is make it easy.

Make it easy.
Make it easy.
Everybody's got something to hide,
Except for me and my monkey.

Come on, come on, come on...

Sexy Sadie

Sexy Sadie, what have you done?
You made a fool of everyone,
You made a fool of everyone.
Sexy Sadie, oh what have you done?

Sexy Sadie, you broke the rules,
You laid it down for all to see,
You laid it down for all to see.
Sexy Sadie, oh, you broke the rules.

One sunny day the world was waiting for a lover,
She came along to turn on everyone.
Sexy Sadie, she's the greatest of them all.

Sexy Sadie, how did you know?
The world was waiting just for you,
The world was waiting just for you.
Sexy Sadie, oh, how did you know?

Sexy Sadie, you'll get yours yet,
However big you think you are,
However big you think you are.
Sexy Sadie, oh you'll get yours yet.

We gave her everything we owned
Just to sit at her table.
Just a smile would lighten everything.
Sexy Sadie, she's the latest and the greatest of them all.

Ooh...

Helter Skelter

When I get to the bottom I go back to the top of the slide,
Where I stop and I turn and I go for a ride,
Till I get to the bottom, and I see you again,
Yeah, yeah, yeah!

Do you, don't you, want me to love you?
I'm coming down fast, but I'm miles above you.
Tell me, tell me, tell me,
Come on, tell me the answer,
Well, you may be a lover, but you ain't no dancer.

Helter Skelter, Helter Skelter,
Helter Skelter, yeah!

Will you, won't you want me to make you?
I'm coming down fast, but don't let me break you.
Tell me, tell me, tell, me the answer,
You may be a lover, but you ain't no dancer.

Look out!
Helter Skelter, Helter Skelter,
Helter Skelter, yeah!

Look out! 'Cause here she comes!

When I get to the bottom I go back to the top of the slide,
Where I stop and I turn and I go for a ride,
Till I get to the bottom, and I see you again,
Yeah, yeah, yeah!

Well, do you, don't you want me to make you?
I'm coming down fast, but don't let me break you.
Tell me, tell me, tell me your answer,
You may be a lover, but you ain't no dancer.

Look out!
Helter Skelter, Helter Skelter,
Helter Skelter, yeah!

Look out! Helter Skelter!
She coming down fast!
Yes she is,
Yes she is
Coming down fast...

Long Long Long

It's been a long, long, long time.
How could I ever have lost you,
When I loved you?
It took a long, long, long time.

Now I'm so happy I found you,
How I love you.

So many tears I was searching,
So many tears I was wasting,
Oh, Oh!

Now I can see you,
Be you.

How can I ever misplace you?
How I want you.
How I love you.
You know that I need you.
Oh, I love you.

Honey Pie

She was a working girl,
North of England way.
Now she's hit the big time
In the USA.
And if she could only hear me,
This is what I'd say:

Honey pie, you are making me crazy,
I'm in love, but I'm lazy,
So won't you please come home?

Oh, honey pie, my position is tragic,
Come and show me the magic
Of your Hollywood song.

You became a legend of the silver screen,
And now the thought of meeting you
Makes me weak in the knee.

Oh, honey pie, you are driving me frantic,
Sail across the Atlantic
To be where you belong.
Honey pie, come back to me.

(... I like this kind of hot kind of music,
Hot kind of music,
Play it to me,
Play it to me, Hollywood blues)

Will the wind that blew her boat across the sea
Kindly send her sailing back to me.

Now, Honey pie, you are making me crazy,
I'm in love, but I'm lazy,
So won't you please come home.

(Come, come back to me Honey Pie...
Honey Pie, Honey Pie)

Savoy Truffle

Cream tangerine and montelimat,
A ginger sling with a pineapple heart,
A coffee dessert, yes, you know it's good news,
But you'll have to have them all pulled out
After the Savoy truffle.

Cool cherry cream, nice apple tart.
I feel your taste all the time we're apart,
Coconut fudge really blows down those blues,
But you'll have to have them all pulled out
After the Savoy truffle.

You might not feel it now,
But when the pain cuts through,
You're going to know, and how.
The sweat is gonna fill your head,
When it becomes too much, you'll shout aloud...

But you'll have to have them all pulled out
After the Savoy truffle.

You know that what you eat you are,
But what is sweet now, turns so sour.
We all know Ob-la-di-bla-da,
But can you show me where you are?

Cream tangerine and montelimat,
A ginger sling with a pineapple heart,
Coffee dessert, yes, you know it's good news,
But you'll have to have them all pulled out
After the savoy truffle.
Yes, you'll have to have them all pulled out
After the savoy truffle.

Cry Baby Cry

Cry baby cry,
Make your mother sigh,
She's old enough to know better.

The King of Marigold
Was in the kitchen
Cooking breakfast for the Queen.
The Queen was in the parlour,
Playing piano
For the children of the King.

Cry baby cry,
Make your mother sigh,
She's old enough to know better,
So cry baby cry.

The King was in the garden,
Picking flowers for a friend
Who came to play.
The Queen was in the playroom,
Painting pictures
For the children's holiday.

Cry baby cry,
Make your mother sigh,
She's old enough to know better,
So cry baby cry.

The Duchess of Kirkaldy,
Always smiling,
And arriving late for tea.
The Duke was having problems
With a message
At the local Bird and Bee.

Cry baby cry,
Make your mother sigh,
She's old enough to know better,
So cry baby cry.

At twelve o'clock a meeting
Round the table

For a seance in the dark.
With voices out of nowhere,
Put on specially
By the children, for a lark.

Cry baby cry,
Make your mother sigh,
She's old enough to know better,
So cry baby cry.

Cry, cry, cry baby,
Make your mother sigh,
She's old enough to know better,
So cry baby cry.

Cry, cry, cry,
Make your mother sigh,
She's old enough to know better,
So cry baby cry.

Good Night

Now it's time to say good night
Good night, sleep tight.
Now the sun turns out his light,
Good night, sleep tight.

Dream sweet dreams for me,
Dream sweet dreams for you.

Close your eyes and I'll close mine,
Good night, sleep tight.
Now the moon begins to shine
Good night, sleep tight.

Dream sweet dreams for me,
Dream sweet dreams for you.

Mm-mm-mm...

Close your eyes and I'll close mine,
Good night, sleep tight.
Now the sun turns out his light,
Good night, sleep tight.

Dream sweet dreams for me,
Dream sweet dreams for you.

Good night,
Good night everybody,
Everybody everywhere,
Good night.

Only A Northern Song

If you're listening to this song,
You may think the chords are going wrong.
But they're not –
We just wrote it like that.

When you're listening late at night,
You may think the band are not quite right.
But they are –
They just play it like that.

It doesn't really matter what chords I play,
What words I say,
Or time of day it is,
'Cause it's only a Northern song.

It doesn't really matter what clothes I wear,
Or how I fare,
Of if my hair is brown,
When it's only a Northern Song.

If you think the harmony
Is a little dark and out of key.
You're correct –
There's nobody there.

And I told you there's no-one there.

All Together Now

One, two, three, four,
Can I have a little more?
Five, six, seven, eight, nine, ten,
I love you.

A, B, C, D,
Can I bring my friend to tea?
E, F, G, H, I, J,
I love you.

Sail the ship,
Chop the tree,
Skip the rope,
Look at me!

All together now, all together now,
All together now, all together now.

Black, white, green, red,
Can I take my friend to bed?
Pink, brown, yellow, orange and blue,
I love you.

All together now, all together now,
All together now, all together now,
All together now, all together now,
All together now, all together now.

Sail the ship,
Chop the tree,
Skip the rope,
Look at me!

All together now, all together now,
All together now, all together now,
All together now, all together now,
All together now, all together now,
All together now, all together now,
All together now, all together now!

Hey Bulldog

Sheep dog standing in the rain,
Bullfrog, doing it again.
Some kind of happiness
Is measured out in miles.
What makes you think you're something
Special when you smile?

Child-like, no one understands,
Jackknife in your sweaty hands.
Some kind of innocence
Is measured out in years,
You don't know what it's like
To listen to your fears.

You can talk to me,
You can talk to me,
You can talk to me,
If you're lonely, you can talk to me.

Big man, walking in the park,
Wigwam, frightened of the dark.
Some kind of solitude
Is measured out in you.
You think you know me,
But you haven't got a clue.

You can talk to me,
You can talk to me,
You can talk to me,
If you're lonely, you can talk to me.

Hey bulldog! Hey bulldog!
Hey bulldog! Hey bulldog!

(Hey, man.
What's that, boy?
Woof!
What'd you say?
I said, Woof!
D'you know any more?
Wowu-wa!
Ah hah-hah!...)

It's All Too Much

It's all too much.
It's all too much.

When I look into your eyes,
Your love is there for me.
And the more I go inside,
The more there is to see.

It's all too much for me to take,
The love that's shining all around you.
Everywhere, it's what you make,
For us to take, it's all too much.

Floating down the stream of time
From life to life with me.
Makes no difference where you are,
Or where you'd like to be.

It's all too much for me to take,
The love that's shining all around here.
All the world is birthday cake,
So take a piece, but not too much.

Sail me on a silver sun
Where I know that I'm free.
Show me that I'm everywhere,
And get me home for tea.

It's all too much for me to see,
The love that's shining all around here,
The more I learn, the less I know,
And once I do, it's all too much.

It's all too much for me to take
The love that's shining all around you
Everywhere, it's what you make,
For us to take, it's all too much.

It's too much.
Ah...
It's too much.

With your long blonde hair and your eyes of blue...
With your long blonde hair and your eyes of blue...

You're too much ah...

Too much, too much,
Too much, too much,
Too much, too much,
Too much, too much...

Get Back

Jojo was a man who thought he was a loner,
But he knew it couldn't last.
Jojo left his home in Tucson, Arizona,
For some California grass.

Get back, get back,
Get back to where you once belonged.
Get back, get back,
Get back to where you once belonged.

Get back Jojo...
Go home.

Get back, get back,
Back to where you once belonged.
Get back, get back,
Back to where you once belonged.

Get back Jo!

Sweet Loretta Martin thought she was a woman,
But she was another man.
All the girls around her say she's got it coming,
But she gets it while she can.

Oh get back, get back,
Get back to where you once belonged.
Get back, get back,
Get back to where you once belonged.

Get back Loretta...
Go home.

Oh get back, you get back,
Get back to where you once belonged.
You get back, get back,
Get back to where you once belonged...
Ooh.

Get back Loretta,
Your mommy's waiting for you,
Wearing her high-heel shoes,

And her low-neck sweater,
Get back home, Loretta.

Get back, get back,
Get back to where you once belonged...

Don't Let Me Down

Don't let me down,
Don't let me down,
Don't let me down,
Don't let me down.

Nobody ever loved me like she does,
Ooh she does, yes she does.
And if somebody loved me
Like she do me,
Ooh she do me, yes she does.

Don't let me down,
Don't let me down,
Don't let me down,
Don't let me down.

I'm in love for the first time,
Don't you know it's going to last.
It's a love that lasts forever,
It's a love that has no past.

Don't let me down,
Don't let me down,
Don't let me down,
Don't let me down.

And from the first time
That she really done me.
Ooh, she done me,
She done me good.
I guess nobody ever really done me,
Ooh she done me,
She done me good.

Don't let me down,
Hey! Don't let me down...
Don't let me down...

The Ballad Of John And Yoko

Standing in the dock at Southampton,
Trying to get to Holland or France.
The man in the mac said,
You've got to go back,
You know they didn't even give us a chance.

Christ! You know it ain't easy,
You know how hard it can be.
The way things are going,
They're going to crucify me.

Finally made the plane into Paris,
Honeymooning down by the Seine.
Peter Brown called to say,
You can make it OK,
You can get married in Gibraltar, near Spain.

Christ! You know it ain't easy,
You know how hard it can be.
The way things are going,
They're going to crucify me.

Drove from Paris to the Amsterdam Hilton,
Talking in our beds for a week.
The newspeople said,
Say, what you doing in bed?
I said, We're only trying to get us some peace.

Christ! You know it ain't easy,
You know how hard it can be.
The way things are going,
They're going to crucify me.

Saving up your money for a rainy day,
Giving all your clothes to charity.
Last night the wife said,
Oh boy, when you're dead,
You don't take nothing with you but your soul –
Think!

Made a lightning trip to Vienna,
Eating chocolate cake in a bag.

The newspapers said,
She's gone to his head,
They look just like two gurus in drag.

Christ! You know it ain't easy,
You know how hard it can be.
The way things are going,
They're going to crucify me.

Caught the early plane back to London,
Fifty acorns tied in a sack.
The men from the press said,
We wish you success,
It's good to have the both of you back.

Christ! You know it ain't easy,
You know how hard it can be.
The way things are going,
They're going to crucify me.
The way things are going,
They're going to crucify me.

Old Brown Shoe

I want a love that's right,
But right is only half of what's wrong.
I want a short-haired girl
Who sometimes wears it twice as long.

Now I'm stepping out this old brown shoe,
Baby, I'm in love with you,
I'm so glad you came here,
It won't be the same now, I'm telling you.

You know, you pick me up from where
Some tried to drag me down.
And when I see your smile
Replacing every thoughtless frown.

You've got me escaping from this zoo,
Baby, I'm in love with you,
I'm so glad you came here,
It won't be the same now, I'm telling you.

If I grow up, I'll be a singer,
Wearing rings on every finger,
Not worrying what they or you say.
I'll live and love and maybe some day,
Who knows, baby,
You may comfort me.

I may appear to be imperfect,
My love is something you can't reject,
I'm changing faster than the weather,
If you and me should get together,
Who knows, baby,
You may comfort me.

I want that love of yours,
To miss that love is something I'd hate.
I'll make an early start,
I'm making sure that I'm not late.

For your sweet top lip I'm in the queue,
Baby, I'm in love with you,
I'm so glad you came here,

It won't be the same now when I'm with you.
I'm so glad you came here,
It won't be the same now when I'm with you.

Come Together

Here come old flat top,
He come grooving up slowly,
He got joo joo eyeball,
He one holy roller,
He got hair down to his knee.
Got to be a joker, he just do what he please.

He wear no shoe shine,
He got toe jam football,
He got monkey finger,
He shoot Coca Cola,
He say, I know you,
You know me.
One thing I can tell you is
You got to be free.

Come together,
Right now,
Over me.

He bag production
He got walrus gumboot,
He got Ono sideboard,
He one spinal cracker,
He got feet down below his knee.
Hold you in his armchair, you can feel his disease.

Come together,
Right now,
Over me.

(Right!...
Come... come)

He roller coaster,
He got early warning,
He got muddy water,
He one mojo filter,
He say, One and one
And one is three.
Got to be good looking
'Cause he's so hard to see.

Come together,
Right now,
Over me.

Oh!
Come together, yeah.
Come together, yeah...

Something

Something in the way she moves
Attracts me like no other lover.
Something in the way she woos me.

I don't want to leave her now,
You know I believe, and how.

Somewhere in her smile she knows
That I don't need no other lover.
Something in her style that shows me.

Don't want to leave her now,
You know I believe, and how.

You're asking me will me love grow,
I don't know, I don't know.
You stick around now, it may show,
I don't know, I don't know.

Something in the way she knows,
And all I have to do is think of her.
Something in the things she shows me.

I don't want to leave her now,
You know I believe, and how.

Maxwell's Silver Hammer

Joan was quizzical,
Studied pataphysical science in the home.
Late night all alone with a test-tube,
Oh, oh-oh oh.
Maxwell Edison, majoring in medicine,
Calls her on the phone:
Can I take you out to the pictures, Joan?
But as she's getting ready to go,
A knock comes on the door.

Bang, bang, Maxwell's silver hammer came down on her head,
Bang, bang, Maxwell's silver hammer made sure that she was dead.

Back in school again, Maxwell plays the fool again,
Teacher gets annoyed.
Wishing to avoid an unpleasant scene,
She tells Max to stay when the class has gone away,
So he waits behind,
Writing fifty times, I must not be so.
But when she turns her back on the boy,
He creeps up from behind.

Bang, bang, Maxwell's silver hammer came down on her head,
Bang, bang, Maxwell's silver hammer made sure that she was dead.

P.C. Thirty-One said, We've caught a dirty one,
Maxwell stands alone,
Painting testimonial pictures,
Oh, oh-oh oh.
Rose and Valerie, screaming from the gallery,
Say he must go free.
The judge does not agree, and he tells them so.
But as the words are leaving his lips,
A noise comes from behind.

Bang, bang, Maxwell's silver hammer came down on his head,
Bang, bang, Maxwell's silver hammer made sure that he was dead.
Wo-wo-woh.

Silver hammer man.

Oh! Darling

Oh! darling, please believe me,
I'll never do you no harm.
Believe me when I tell you,
I'll never do you no harm.

Oh! darling, if you leave me,
I'll never make it alone.
Believe me when I beg you,
Don't ever leave me alone.

When you told me you didn't need me anymore,
Well, you know I nearly broke down and cried.
When you told me you didn't need me anymore,
Well, you know I nealy broke down and died.

Oh! darling, if you leave me,
I'll never make it alone.
Believe me when I tell you,
I'll never do you no harm.

(Believe me, darling)
When you told me you didn't need me anymore,
Well, you know I nearly broke down and cried.
When you told me you didn't need me anymore,
Well, you know I nearly broke down and died.

Oh! darling, please believe me,
I'll never let you down
(Oh, believe me darling)
Believe me when I tell you,
I'll never do you no harm.

Octopus's Garden

I'd like to be under the sea,
In an octopus's garden in the shade.
He'd let us in, knows where we've been,
In his octopus's garden in the shade.
I'd ask my friends to come and see
An octopus's garden with me.
I'd like to be under the sea
In an octopus's garden in the shade.

We would be warm below the storm
In our little hideaway beneath the waves.
Resting our head on the sea bed
In an octopus's garden near a cave.
We would sing and dance around,
Because we know we can't be found.
I'd like to be under the sea
In an octopus's garden in the shade.

We would shout and swim about
The coral that lies beneath the waves.
Oh, what joy for every girl and boy,
Knowing they're happy and they're safe.
We would be so happy, you and me,
No one there to tell us what to do.
I'd like to be under the sea in an octopus's garden with you,
In an octopus's garden with you,
In an octopus's garden with you.

I Want You (She's So Heavy)

I want you,
I want you so bad,
I want you,
I want you so bad,
It's driving me mad, it's driving me mad.

I want you,
I want you so bad, babe,
I want you,
I want you so bad, it's driving me mad,
It's driving me mad.

I want you,
I want you so bad, babe,
I want you,
I want you so bad,
It's driving me mad, it's driving me mad.

I want you,
I want you so bad,
I want you,
I want you so bad, it's driving me mad,
It's driving me...

She's so... heavy,
Heavy.

She's so... heavy,
Heavy.

I want you,
I want you so bad,
I want you,
I want you so bad,
It's driving me mad, it's driving me mad.

I want you,
You know, I want you so bad, babe
I want you,
You know, I want you so bad, it's driving me mad,
It's driving me mad.
Yeeaaahh!
She's so...

Here Comes The Sun

Here comes the sun,
Here comes the sun,
And I say it's all right.

Little darling, it's been a long, cold, lonely winter.
Little darling, it feels like years since it's been here.

Here comes the sun,
Here comes the sun,
And I say it's all right.

Little darling, the smile's returning to their faces,
Little darling, it seems like years since it's been here.

Here comes the sun,
Here comes the sun,
And I say it's all right.

Sun, sun, sun, here it comes.
Sun, sun, sun, here it comes.
Sun, sun, sun, here it comes.
Sun, sun, sun, here it comes.
Sun, sun, sun, here it comes.

Little darling, I feel that ice is slowly melting,
Little darling, it seems like years since it's been clear.

Here comes the sun,
Here comes the sun,
And I say it's all right.

Here comes the sun,
Here comes the sun,
It's all right,
It's all right.

Because

Ah...

Because the world is round, it turns me on.
Because the world is round.
Ah...

Because the wind is high, it blows my mind.
Because the wind is high.
Ah...

Love is old, love is new,
Love is all, love is you.

Because the sky is blue, it makes me cry.
Because the sky is blue.
Ah...

You Never Give Me Your Money

You never give me your money,
You only give me your funny paper,
And in the middle of negotiations, I break down.

I never give you my number,
I only give you my situation,
And in the middle of investigation, I break down.

Out of college, money spent,
See no future, pay no rent
All the money's gone, nowhere to go.

Any jobber got the sack,
Monday morning turning back,
Yellow lorry slow, nowhere to go.

But oh, that magic feeling, nowhere to go!
Oh, that magic feeling, nowhere to go,
Nowhere to go!
(Ah...)

One sweet dream,
Pick up the bags and get in the limousine.
Soon we'll be away from here,
Step on the gas and wipe that tear away,
One sweet dream came true today,
Came true today,
Came true today,
Yes it did...

One two three four, five, six, seven,
All good children go to heaven...

Sun King

Ah...

Here come the Sun King,
Here come the Sun King,
Everybody's laughing,
Everybody's happy,
Here come the Sun King.

Quando paramucho mi amore defelice corazon,
Mundo paparazzi mi amore chicka ferdy parasol,
Cuesto obrigado tanta mucho que can eat it carousel.

Mean Mr. Mustard

Mean Mr. Mustard sleeps in the park,
Shaves in the dark
Trying to save paper.
Sleeps in a hole in the road.
Saving up to buy some clothes.
Keeps a ten bob note up his nose,
Such a mean old man,
Such a mean old man.

His sister Pam works in a shop,
She never stops,
She's a go-getter.
Takes him out to look at the Queen,
Only place that he's ever been,
Always shouts out something obscene,
Such a dirty old man, dirty old man.

Polythene Pam

Well, you should see Polythene Pam,
She's so good looking, but she looks like a man.
Well, you should see her in drag,
Dressed in her polythene bag,
Yes, you should see Polythene Pam –
Yeah, yeah, yeah.

Get a dose of her in jackboots and kilt,
She's killer diller when she's dressed to the hilt.
She's the kind of a girl
That makes the News of the World,
Yes, you could say she was attractively built.
Yeah, yeah, yeah.

She Came in Through The Bathroom Window

She came in through the bathroom window,
Protected by a silver spoon.
But now she sucks her thumb and wonders
By the banks of her own lagoon.

Didn't anybody tell her?
Didn't anybody see?
Sundays on the phone to Monday,
Tuesdays on the phone to me.

She said she'd always been a dancer,
She worked at fifteen clubs a day,
And though she thought I knew the answer,
Well, I knew what I could not say.

And so I quit the police department,
And got myself a steady job.
And though she tried her best to help me,
She could steal, but she could not rob.

Didn't anybody tell her?
Didn't anybody see?
Sundays on the phone to Monday,
Tuesdays on the phone to me,
Oh yeah.

Golden Slumbers

Once there was a way to get back homeward,
Once there was a way to get back home.
Sleep pretty darling, do not cry,
And I will sing a lullaby.

Golden slumbers fill your eyes,
Smiles awake you when you rise.
Sleep pretty darling, do not cry,
And I will sing a lullaby.

One there was a way to get back homeward,
Once there was a way to get back home.
Sleep pretty darling, do not cry,
And I will sing a lullaby.

Carry That Weight

Boy, you're gonna carry that weight,
Carry that weight a long time.
Boy, you're gonna carry that weight,
Carry that weight a long time.

I never give you my pillow,
I only send you my invitations,
And in the middle of the celebrations
I break down.

Boy, you're gonna carry that weight,
Carry that weight a long time.
Boy, you're gonna carry that weight,
Carry that weight a long time.

The End

Oh yeah! All right!
Are you gonna be in my dreams tonight?

Love you, love you,
Love you, love you,
Love you, love you,
Love you, love you...

And in the end,
The love you take
Is equal to the love you make.
Ah...

Her Majesty

Her Majesty's a pretty nice girl,
But she doesn't have a lot to say.
Her Majesty's a pretty nice girl,
But she changes from day to day.
I wanna tell her that I love her a lot,
But I gotta get a belly full of wine.
Her Majesty's a pretty nice girl,
Some day I'm gonna make her mine, oh yeah,
Some day I'm gonna make her mine.

Let It Be

When I find myself in times of trouble,
Mother Mary comes to me,
Speaking words of wisdom, let it be.

And in my hour of darkness,
She is standing right in front of me,
Speaking words of wisdom, let it be.

Let it be, let it be,
Let it be, let it be,
Whisper words of wisdom, let it be.

And when the broken-hearted people
Living in the world agree,
There will be an answer, let it be.

For though they may be parted,
There is still a chance that they will see
There will be an answer, let it be.

Let it be, let it be,
Let it be, let it be.
Yeah, there will be an answer, let it be.

Let it be, let it be,
Let it be, let it be.
Whisper words of wisdom, let it be.

Let it be, let it be,
Let it be, yeah let it be.
Whisper words of wisdom, let it be.

And when the night is cloudy,
There is still a light that shines on me,
Shine until tomorrow, let it be.

I wake up to the sound of music,
Mother Mary comes to me,
Speaking words of wisdom, let it be.

Yeah, let it be, let it be,
Let it be, yeah, let it be.

There will be an answer, let it be.

Let it be, let it be,
Let it be, yeah, let it be.
There will be an answer, let it be.

Let it be, let it be,
Let it be, yeah, let it be.
Whisper words of wisdom, let it be.

You Know My Name (Look Up The Number)

You know my name,
Look up the number.
You know my name,
Look up the number.
You, you know, you know my name,
You, you know, you know my name.

Good evening and welcome to Slaggers,
Featuring Denis O'Bell.
... Ringo, Hey, Ringo!
Let's hear it for Denis! Ha-hay!

Good evening –
You know my name,
Better look up my number.
You know my name –
That's right – look up my number.

You, you know, you know my name,
You, you know, you know my name,
You know my name
Ba-ba-ba-ba-ba-ba-ba-ba-pum
Look up my number.
You know my name... hah!
That's right – look up the number.

Oh, you know, you know,
You know my name,
You know, you know,
You know my name.
Huh huh huh huh,
You know my name,
Ba-ba-ba-pum,
Look up the number.
You know my name,
Look up the number.

You, you know, you know my name, baby,
You, you know, you know my name,
You know, you know my name,
You know, you know my name.

Oh let's hear it!
Go on, Denis, let's hear it for Denis O'Bell!

You know, you know, you know my name,
You know, you know, you know my name.
You know my name, look up the number,
You know my name, look up the number,
You know my name, look up the number.

You know my number one, you know my number two,
You know my number three, and you know my number four,
You know my name,
You know my number too,
You know my name you know my number,
What's up with you? Ha!

You know my name,
That's right.

Yeah...

Two Of Us

Two of us riding nowhere,
Spending someone's hard-earned pay.
You and me Sunday driving,
Not arriving on our way back home.

We're on our way home,
We're on our way home,
We're going home.

Two of us sending postcards,
Writing letters on my wall.
You and me burning matches,
Lifting latches,
On our way back home.

We're on our way home,
We're on our way home,
We're going home.

You and I have memories,
Longer than the road that stretches out ahead.

Two of us wearing raincoats,
Standing solo in the sun.
You and me chasing paper,
Getting nowhere,
On our way back home,

We're on our way home,
We're on our way home,
We're going home.

You and I have memories,
Longer than the road that stretches out ahead.

Two of us wearing raincoats,
Standing solo in the sun.
You and me chasing paper,
Getting nowhere,
On our way back home,

We're on our way home,
We're on our way home,
We're going home.

Dig A Pony

I dig a pony,
Well, you can celebrate anything you want,
Yes, you can celebrate anything you want,
Oh!

I do a road hog,
Well, you can penetrate any place you go,
Yes, you can penetrate any place you go,
I told you so.

All I want is you,
Everything has got to be just like you want it to.
Because...

I pick a moondog,
Well, you can radiate everything you are,
Yes, you can radiate everything you are,

Oh, now
I roll a stoney,
Well, you can imitate everyone you know,
Yes, you can imitate everyone you know,
I told you so.

All I want is you.
Everything has got to be just like you want it to.
Because...

Oh now,
I feel the wind blow.
Well, you can indicate everything you see,
Yes, you can indicate anything you see.

Oh now,
I cold and lonely
Well, you can syndicate any boat you row.
Yeah, you can syndicate any boat you row.
I told you so.

All I want is you.
Everything has got to be just like you want it to.
Because...

Across The Universe

Words are flowing out
Like endless rain into a paper cup,
They slither while they pass,
They slip away across the universe.
Pools of sorrow, waves of joy
Are drifting through my opened mind,
Possessing and caressing me.

Jai Guru Deva Om.
Nothing's gonna change my world,
Nothing's gonna change my world.
Nothing's gonna change my world,
Nothing's gonna change my world.

Images of broken light
Which dance before me like a million eyes,
They call me on and on, across the universe.
Thoughts meander like a restless wind
Inside a letter box,
They tumble blindly as they make
Their way across the universe.

Jai Guru Deva Om.
Nothing's gonna change my world,
Nothing's gonna change my world.
Nothing's gonna change my world,
Nothing's gonna change my world.

Sounds of laughter, shades of earth
Are ringing through my opened ears,
Inciting and inviting me.
Limitless undying love,
Which shines around me like a million suns
It calls me on and on across the universe.

Jai Guru Deva Om.
Nothing's gonna change my world,
Nothing's gonna change my world.
Nothing's gonna change my world,
Nothing's gonna change my world.

Jai Guru Deva, Jai Guru Deva,
Jai Guru Deva, Jai Guru Deva...

I Me Mine

All through the day,
I me mine, I me mine, I me mine.
All through the night,
I me mine, I me mine, I me mine.

Never frightened of leaving it,
Everyone's weaving it,
Coming on strong all the time.
All through the day,
I me mine.

I me-me mine, I me-me mine,
I me-me mine, I me-me mine.

All I can hear,
I me mine, I me mine, I me mine.
Even those tears,
I me mine, I me mine, I me mine.

No one's frightened of playing it,
Everyone's saying it,
Flowing more freely than wine.
All through the day,
I me mine.

I me-me mine, I me-me mine,
I me-me mine, I me-me mine.

All I can hear,
I me mine, I me mine, I me mine.
Even those tears,
I me mine, I me mine, I me mine.

No one's frightened of playing it,
Everyone's saying it,
Flowing more freely than wine.
All through your life,
I me mine.

Dig It

... Like a rolling stone,
Like a rolling stone,
Like the FBI,
And the CIA,
And the BBC... BB King,
And Doris Day,
Matt Busby,
Dig it, dig it,
Dig it, dig it,
Dig it, dig it,
Dig it, dig it...

I've Got A Feeling

I've got a feeling, a feeling deep inside,
Oh yeah, oh yeah.
I've got a feeling, a feeling I can't hide,
Oh no, oh no,
Oh no.
Yeah, yeah! I've got a feeling.

Oh, please believe me,
I'd hate to miss the train,
Oh yeah, oh yeah.
And if you leave me, I won't be late again,
Oh no, oh no,
Oh no.
Yeah, yeah! I've got a feeling, yeah!

All these years I've been wandering around,
Wondering how come nobody told me
All that I've been looking for was
Somebody who looked like you.

I've got a feeling that keeps me on my toes,
Oh yeah, oh yeah.
I've got a feeling,
I think that everybody knows,
Oh yeah, oh yeah,
Oh yeah.
Yeah, yeah! I've got a feeling, yeah!

Everybody had a hard year,
Everybody had a good time,
Everybody had a wet dream
Everybody saw the sunshine,
Oh yeah, oh yeah,
Oh yeah.

Everybody had a good year,
Everybody let their hair down
Everybody pulled their socks up,
Everybody put their foot down,
Oh yeah.

(Repeat first verse and last two verses.)

One After 909

My baby says she's travelling
On the One after 909.
I said, Move over, honey,
I'm travelling on that line.
I said, Move over once,
Move over twice,
Come on baby, don't be cold as ice.
Said she's travelling
On the One after 909.

I begged her not to go,
And I begged her on my bended knee.
You're only fooling around,
Only fooling around with me.
I said, Move over once,
Move over twice,
Come on baby, don't be cold as ice.
Said she's travelling
On the One after 909.

Pick up my bags,
Run to the station.
Railman says, You've got the wrong location.
Pick up my bag,
Run right home,
Then I find I've got the number wrong.

Well, said she's travelling
On the One after 909.
I said, Move over, honey,
I'm travelling on that line.
I said, Move over once,
Move over twice,
Come on baby, don't be cold as ice.
Said she's travelling on the One after 909.

Pick up my bags,
Run to the station.
Railman says, You've got the wrong location.
Pick up my bag,
Run right home,
Then I find I've got the number wrong.

Well, she says she's travelling
On the One after 909.
I said, Move over, honey,
I'm travelling on that line.
I said, Move over once,
Move over twice,
Come on baby, don't be cold as ice.
Said she's travelling on the One after 9-0
She said she's travelling on the One after 9-0
Said she's travelling on the One after 909.

The Long And Winding Road

The long and winding road,
That leads to your door
Will never disappear.
I've seen that road before.
It always leads me here –
Lead me to your door.

The wild and windy night
That the rain washed away,
Has left a pool of tears crying for the day.
Why leave me standing here?
Let me know the way.

Many times I've been alone,
And many times I've cried,
Anyway, you'll never know
The many ways I've tried.

And still they lead me back
To the long, winding road.
You left me standing here
A long, long time ago.
Don't leave me waiting here –
Lead me to your door.

But still they lead me back,
To the long, winding road.
You left me standing here
A long, long time ago.
Don't keep me waiting here –
Lead me to your door.
(Yeah, yeah, yeah, yeah.)

For You Blue

Because you're sweet and lovely, girl, I love you.
Because you're sweet and lovely, girl, it's true.
I love you more than ever, girl, I do.

I want you in the morning, girl, I love you.
I want you at the moment I feel blue,
I'm living every moment, girl, for you.

I've loved you from the moment I saw you.
You looked at me, that's all you had to do.
I feel it now, I hope you feel it too.

Because you're sweet and lovely, girl, I love you.
Because you're sweet and lovely, girl, it's true.
I love you more than ever, girl, I do.

Christmas Time (Is Here Again)

Christmas time is here again,
Christmas time is here again,
Christmas time is here again,
Christmas time is here again,
O-U-T spells 'out'...

In Spite Of All The Danger

In spite of all the danger,
In spite of all that may be,
I'll do anything for you,
Anything you want me to,
If you'll be true to me.

In spite of all the heartache
That you may cause me,
I'll do anything for you,
Anything you want me to,
If you'll be true to me.

I'll look after you like I've never done before,
I'll keep all the others from knocking at your door.

In spite of all the danger,
In spite of all that may be,
I'll do anything for you,
Anything you want me to,
If you'll be true to me.

In spite of all the heartache
That you may cause me,
I'll do anything for you,
Anything you want me to,
If you'll be true to me.
I'll do anything for you,
Anything you want me to,
If you'll be true to me.

You'll Be Mine

When the stars fall at night, you'll be mine...
You'll be mine, until you die,
You'll be mine.

And so all the night, you'll be mine, you'll be mine
And the stars gonna shine, you'll be mine.
Now...

My darling,
When you brought me that toast the other morning,
I, I looked into your eyes and I could see
A National Health eyeball
And I loved you like I have never done,
I have never done before.

Yes, the stars gonna shine
And you'll be mine, and you'll be mine.
You'll be mine, and the stars gonna shine.

Like Dreamers Do

I, I saw a girl in my dreams,
And so it seems that I will love her.
Oh you, you are that girl in my dreams,
And so it seems that I will love you.

And I waited for your kiss,
Waited for the bliss
Like dreamers do.

And I,
Oh, I'll be there, yeah, waiting for you.

You, you came just one dream ago,
And now I know that I will love you.

Oh, I knew when you first said hello,
That's how I know that I will love you.

And I waited for your kiss,
Waited for the bliss,
Like dreamers do.

And I,
Oh, I'll be there, yeah, waiting for you.

You, you came just one dream ago,
And now I know that I will love you.

Oh, I knew when you first said hello,
That's how I know that I will love you.

And I waited for your kiss,
Waited for the bliss
Like dreamers do,
Oh, like dreamers do,
Like dreamers do.

Hello Little Girl

Hello little girl,
Hello little girl,
Hello little girl.

When I see you every day
I say, mm-mm, Hello little girl.
When you're passing on your way
I say, mm-mm, Hello little girl.

When I see you passing by,
I cry mm-mm, Hello little girl
When I try to catch your eye,
I cry mm-mm, Hello little girl.

I send you flowers, but you don't care,
You never seem to see me standing there.
I often wonder what you're thinking of,
I hope it's me – love, love, love.

So I hope there'll come when you'll say
Mm-mm, you're my little girl.

It's not the first time that it's happened to me,
It's been a long, lonely time.
And it's so funny, so funny to see
That I'm about to lose my mind.

So I hope there'll come a day when you'll say
Mm-mm, you're my little girl.
Mm-mm, you're my little girl,
Mm-mm, you're my little girl,
Oh yeah, you're my little girl.

You Know What To Do

When I see you, I just don't know what to say,
I like to be with you every hour of the day.
So if you want me,
Just like I need you,
You know what to do.

I watched you walking by, and you looked all alone,
I hope that you won't mind if I walk you back home.
And if you want me,
Just like I need you,
You know what to do.

Just call on me when you're lonely,
I'll keep my love for you only,
I'll call on you if I'm lonely too.

Understand, I'll stay with you every day,
Make you love me more in every way.
So if you want me
Just like I want you
You know what to do.

Just call on me when you're lonely,
I'll keep my love for you only,
I'll call on you if I'm lonely too.

Understand, I'll stay with you every day,
Make you love me more in every way.
So if you want me
Just like I need you
You know what to do.

If You've Got Trouble

If you've got trouble then you've got less trouble than me.
You say you're worried you can't be as worried as me.
You're quite content to be bad,
With all the advantage you had over me,
Just 'cause you're troubled, then don't bring your troubles to me.

I don't think it's funny when you ask for money and things.
Especially when you're standing there wearing diamonds and rings.
You think I'm soft in the head
Well try someone softer instead, pretty thing,
It's not so funny when you know what money can bring.

You better leave me alone, I don't need a thing from you,
You better take yourself home, go and count a ring or two.

If you got trouble then you've got less trouble than me.
You say you're worried you can't be as worried as me.
You're quite content to be bad,
With all the advantage you had over me.
Just 'cause you're troubled then don't bring your troubles to me.
(Oh rock on, anybody!)

You better leave me alone, I don't need a thing from you,
You better take yourself home, go and count a ring or two.

If you got trouble then you've got less trouble than me.
You say you're worried you can't be as worried as me.
You're quite content to be bad
With all the advantage you had over me.
Just 'cause you're troubled, then don't bring your troubles to me.
Just 'cause you're troubled, then don't bring your troubles to me.

That Means A Lot

A friend says that your love won't mean a lot,
But you know that your love is all you've got.
At times, things are so fine,
And at times they're not,
But when she says she loves you, that means a lot.

A friend says that a love is never true.
But you know that does not apply to you.
A touch can mean so much when it's all you've got
And when she says she loves you, that means a lot.

Love can be, deep inside,
Love can be suicide,
Can't you see you can't hide
What you feel when it's real?

A friend says that your love won't mean a lot.
But you know that your love is all you've got.
A touch can mean so much when it's all you've got,
But when she says she loves you, that means a lot.

Can't you see, yeah,
Can't you see, yeah,
Can't you see, yeah...

Not Guilty

Not guilty
Of getting in your way,
While you're trying to steal the day.

Not guilty,
And I'm not before the rest
I'm not trying to steal your vest.

I am not trying to be smart,
I only want what I can get.
I'm really sorry for your ageing head,
But like you heard me say it,

Not guilty.
Though you're signing me a writ
While I'm trying to do my bit.

I don't expect to take your heart,
I only want what I can get.
I'm really sorry that you're underfed,
But like you heard me say it,
Not guilty.

Not guilty
For looking like a freak
Making friends with every Sikh.

Not guilty
For leading you astray
On the road to Mandalay.

I won't upset the apple cart,
I only want what I can get.

I'm really sorry that you've been misled,
But like you heard me say it,
Not guilty.

What's The New Mary Jane?

She looks as an African queen.
She eating twelve chapattis and cream.
She taste as Mongolian lamb.
She coming from Aldeberan.

What a shame Mary Jane had a pain at the party.
What a shame Mary Jane,
What a shame Mary Jane had a pain at the party.

She like to be married with Yeti.
He grooving such cookie spaghetti.
She jumping as Mexican bean,
To make that her body more thin.

What a shame Mary Jane had a pain at the party.
What a shame Mary Jane,
What a shame Mary Jane had a pain at the party.

She catch Patagonian pancakes
With that one and gin party makes.
She having always good contacts
She making with apple and contract.

What a shame Mary Jane had a pain at the party.
What a shame Mary Jane,
What a shame Mary Jane had a pain at the party.
(All together now!)
What a shame Mary Jane had a pain at the party.
What a shame,
What, what a shame Mary Jane had a pain at the party.
What a shame, what a shame,
What a shame Mary Jane had a pain at the party.
What a shame, what a shame, what a shame,
What a shame Mary Jane had a pain at the party...